Robert L.
Aug. 10, 1972

Skillful enlarging can transform a disappointing contact print into a most impressive picture. Compare with Fig. 97.

THE PRACTICAL WAY
TO PERFECT
ENLARGEMENTS

By Joseph Foldes

*All illustrations by
the author*

SOUTH BRUNSWICK
NEW YORK: A. S. BARNES AND CO., INC.
LONDON: THOMAS YOSELOFF LTD

To Judith, my Wife.

Contents

Foreword

Enlarging is important. You must learn to do it well because the prints you make are the end product of all your photographic efforts. *The quality of your prints actually determines the success or failure of* YOU *as a photographer.*

To learn to make top notch enlargements you need:

1. *A complete instruction manual* that teaches a simple and direct system for the production of fine prints. It is in your hands right now. On the outside, this volume may look like just another book on enlarging, in reality it is much more. This book contains all of the techniques you need. The methods described are the result of long experience in enlarging and in the teaching of it. In effect, this book is a complete home study course in enlarging. Never before has this subject been covered so completely or in such a compact and handy form.

2. You must *believe* that *you* can make top quality enlargements *because you can.* Enlarging is basically simple and you can learn it fast. *Believe* that this book teacher you the simplest, most effective, most modern methods of enlarging, *because it does.* However, you will find many "experts" who will tell you otherwise, who will advocate different techniques and even show good prints made by their methods. *Do not listen to them.* True, there are more ways than one to get good results. But jumping from one method to another causes confusion. Use the methods we describe because they comprise a complete system which has proven itself successful.

3. *Determination.* You must decide that you want to learn enlarging and then stick to your decision. Good results will come quickly, but you must not be discouraged if in the very beginning you have difficulties, if everything seems to be so "complicated". Everything will become clear and simple as you go along. There is one fact which you must remember: enlarging is *precision* work. You must do everything precisely according to instructions, you may not change any part of the methods described. This is especially important when you start to get good results. Success may "go to your head" and you may feel that you know enough, or that you know better, and as a result you may start to do things differently. If you do that you are facing confusion and disappointment. On the other hand, if you stick precisely to the techniques described in this book we can practically guarantee that you will become an expert printer within a reasonable length of time.

This does not mean that we are against experimentation. Before you can experiment, however, you must learn the basic techniques, must gain the experience that will enable you to evaluate the results of your experiments. For this reason, resist the urge to try this or that. You will make much faster progress if you do.

In these pages you get practical instructions in their simplest form. Theoretical explanations have been eliminated in order to make the book as compact and handy as possible.

How To Make Good Negatives

The *enlargement* is the *end result* of the photographic process. Thanks to modern films and developers, almost any negative you make will yield an acceptable print, but you need good negatives to turn out top notch prints consistently. Besides, it is easier to print good negatives, they require much less manipulation during enlarging.

There are three factors which influence the printing quality of a negative: density, contrast and grain. Sharpness is also an important factor, but here we take it for granted that your negatives are sharp as a result of careful focusing and lack of camera or subject motion.

Negative Density.

Density actually means "darkness", the degree of translucency of a negative. The darker, the less translucent a negative is, the *more* density it has. The thinner, the more translucent a negative is, the *less* density it has. A negative with high density is usually called heavy or dense, one with little density is referred to as thin. The density of a negative is caused by metallic silver deposited in the emulsion of the film. This silver deposit, on the other hand, is the result of exposure to light and subsequent development. Therefore you can control the density of your negatives by controlling the exposure and development combination.

Negative Contrast.

Contrast means the *difference in density* between different parts of a negative. If there is considerable difference in density between the different parts we speak of a negative of high contrast. If there is little difference in density between the different parts of a negative, we have a negative of little contrast, a "flat" negative.

Negative contrast is the result of differences in subject brightness and lighting, and of the length of development. The more difference there is in subject brightness and lighting, the more contrasty the negatives will be and the longer the negative is developed, the more contrasty it will become. Therefore you can control negative contrast by controlling subject brightness and lighting (where possible), and by developing your negatives for the proper

1 Too dense and too flat.   **2** Normal density but, too flat.   **3** Too thin and too flat.

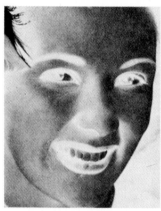  

4-5-6 Negatives of proper density and contrast. Your average negatives should have approximately this quality.

7 Too dense and too contrasty.   **8** Average density but, too contrasty.   **9** Too thin and too contrasty.

length of time. The chemical makeup of the developer also influences negative contrast. There are "contrasty," "normal" and "soft" developers. Figs. 1 to 9 show examples of different negative density and contrast combinations.

Negative Graininess.

The silver deposit in the emulsion is in the form of small particles, uneven in size and shape. If the individual particles show in the enlargement we call the print (and the negative) grainy. The more silver there is present in the emulsion (the denser the negative) the more chance there is that the grain will show in the print. The developer used in processing the negative also controls grain size. Figs. 10 and 11 show examples of prints with coarse and fine grain.

What is a good negative and how can you get one every time?

We cannot show you a negative and say: "Here, this is what all your negatives should look like." Many variations are possible in subject matter, in the conditions under which you take your pictures and in the effect you want to achieve. Still, we can show you a few typical examples and teach you the general principles of good negative making.

Most negatives we see are too dense, too contrasty and usually too grainy. A negative which is a "good printer" is usually rather thin, has medium contrast and negligible grain.

We are using a development method which yields good negatives all the time: *development by inspection.* It is simple, you, too, can use it without any trouble at all and get good negatives consistently.

Desensitizing.

Buy a 15 grain packet of *Ansco Pinakryptol Green,* a quart of denatured

 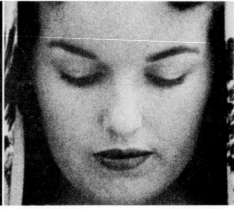

10 Enlargement from a portion of a 35mm negative, which is thin and was developed in a fine grain developer. This shows a fine grain.

11 Enlargement from a portion of a 35mm negative, which is very dense and was developed in a non-fine grain developer. The print shows objectionably coarse grain.

12
Materials needed for making the desensitizer.

alcohol and a supply of distilled water (Fig. 12). Pour 8 oz. of warm distilled water into a dark brown 16 oz. wide necked bottle and dissolve in it the entire 15 grains of the desensitizing dye. When dissolved add 8 oz. of denatured alcohol. This is your desensitizer *stock solution*. To make the *working solution* mix one part of stock solution, one part of denatured alchohol and nine parts of distilled water. Make a sufficient quantity to fill your developing tank or tanks. Pinakryptol Green is an organic dye and as such it can be attacked and spoiled by germs and fungi. The use of distilled water and the addition of alcohol serve to prevent spoilage. As an additional precaution it is best to keep both the stock and working solutions in the refrigerator when not in use (or at least the stock solution). The desensitizer never gets exhausted, you can keep on using it as long as there is a drop of it left. The antihalation backing of the film will discolor the originally dark green solution, but this does not interfere with its action.

In our work we make up a quart of working solution. After each use some of the desensitizer is gone: a little is absorbed by the film, another small amount sticks to the reel and to the inside of the tank. When the remaining amount of desensitizer is not enough to cover the film in the tank we make fresh working solution and add it to the old until the bottle is full. We do this whenever necessary until all the stock solution is gone. When the working solution is not enough to fill the tank and there is no more stock solution left, we simply discard the remaining working solution (it is still potent, but full of sludge and sediment by now), buy another packet of Pinakryptol Green and make fresh solutions. Working it this way one batch of desensitizer usually lasts from six months to a year, depending on the amount of work we do. If you divide the cost of the desensitizer by the number of films desensitized you will find that the expense is negligible.

When the desensitizer has been used a lot it foams readily, but this, like the discoloration caused by the film backing, does not interfere with its working. If you make and use the desensitizer as described, it will never go bad on you (ours has never spoiled yet), but if you do not follow instructions the desensitizer may become spoiled. Spoiled desensitizer has a rotten smell, it usually turns yellow in color and resembles stale beer.

Desensitizing increases developing time but it does not decrease effective film speed.

Why Desensitize?

Film manufacturers advise you to handle negative materials in *total darkness.* If development by inspection is desired they recommend the use of a safelight equipped with a dark green filter for panchromatic films, or a dark red filter for orthochromatic films. The recommended safelights supply very little light and even this small amount will fog the film if it is held too close to the safelight or is inspected too long.

To judge negative density properly during development you need more light to see by and more time for inspection than is possible without desensitization.

As its name implies, desensitizing renders the film less sensitive to light, it enables you to inspect the film during development for somewhat longer periods by the comparatively bright light of the yellow-green safelight used for enlarging.

Desensitizing and development by inspection are not limited by negative size. We desensitize and develop by inspection every negative we make, mostly 35 mm, 120 and 4x5" sizes. Occasionally we also develop subminiature (16 mm) films and larger sheet film sizes. Regardless of size, desensitizing and development by inspection always helps you to get good quality negatives.

Developers to Use.

You should use a soft working, fine grain developer. Most difficulties during printing are caused by excessive negative contrast. Edwal's *Minicol* is an excellent, soft working, fine grain developer, you should use it for your small negatives (up to 2¼x2¼"). Ansco's *Finex-L* is also very good, it yields somewhat more contrasty results than *Minicol*. Negatives developed in Kodak's *Microdol* will have still more contrast. For 4x5" and larger films use the developer recommended by the manufacturer of the film.

Step by Step Description of Development by Inspection.

1. Load the film in the tank as you usually do.
2. Pour in the desensitizer (working solution), it should be about 68°F. (Fig. 13).

13 Desensitizer is poured into tank.

14 Agitate film in desensitizer.

15 Pour desensitizer out of developing tank.

16 Pour in developer.

3. Agitate the film rather vigorously for about 5 minutes (Fig. 14).

4. Pour off the desensitizer (Fig. 15). Do not rinse. The developer will become greenish in time from the desensitizer left in the tank, but this does no harm.

5. Pour in the developer (Fig. 16). Make sure that it is at the right temperature as recommended by the manufacturer of the developer and/or of the film you use. Maintain proper temperature during developing, place the tank in a water bath if necessary. The water bath consists of a container (usually a tray) filled with water. The tank is placed in the water, the temperature of which is adjusted by the addition of ice or hot water, depending on whether a downward or upward change in temperature is necessary. For best results the water level in the container should match approximately the level of developer inside the tank.

6. After about half of the usual developing time has elapsed you can open the tank and inspect the film by the comparatively bright light of a Wratten OA, Ansco A6 or similar yellowish green safelight equipped with a 10 Watt bulb. Hold the film about 2½ feet away from the safelight. Lift out the reel, let the developer drain back into the tank. Put your index finger under the edge of the film and pull it up (Fig. 17). Peel off a short length of film (a few frames) and *look at the emulsion side* (inside) of the film on the reel) (Fig. 18). Do *not* look through the film. After some practice you will be able to judge negative density by looking at the emulsion side of the film under the safelight. After inspection replace the film on the reel. To do it pinch the film gently by the edges, hold it somewhat arched while the other hand turns the reel, pulling the film from between your fingers (Fig. 19). Put the reel back into the tank and replace the cover. Continue developing,

agitate regularly. After a few minutes inspect the film again the same way as before. Continue developing and inspect the film at regular intervals. Development is completed when you find that negative density is just what you want it to be.

7. Pour the developer back into its bottle with the help of a clean funnel (Fig. 20).

8. Pour cold water (about 68°F) into tank, (Fig. 21) agitate it a few times, then pour the water off (Fig. 22).

9. Pour in hypo (Fig. 23). Use fresh hypo containing hardener. Agitate film often during fixation, leave it in hypo for about 15 minutes, then pour hypo back (Fig. 24).

10. Wash films in *filtered* running water (Fig. 25). Filtering is important because most water supplies contain impurities which settle on the film and later dry into the emulsion, causing an unnecessary amount of print spotting. Suitable water filters are available in most photo supply stores. There are several types. Some use a felt disc filter held between two perforated metal discs. The felt is to be replaced after each use. Other filters contain porous granules of a special plastic. The accumulated dirt can be rinsed out of this type and the filter used again. Your photo supply store will be able to sell you a good filter. Stores selling laboratory equipment also carry a line of good water filters. In any event, do not use water filters or splash preventers containing a few layers of wire mesh. They are not satisfactory for our purpose.

The film is to be washed for about 35 minutes. About every 5 minutes take hold of the reel and give it a vigorous shaking with an up and down motion (Fig. 26). This removes the air bubbles sticking to the film and results in more efficient washing.

11. Remove the washed film from the reel, hang it up to dry with the help of a clothespin. Use clothespins sold in photo supply stores, not the regular household kind. They are better, have a stronger grip. Fold over edge of film before attaching clothespin. If you have any trouble with the film's slipping out of the clothespin, use stainless steel film clips, which take a slipproof grip on the film.

Attach another clothespin to the bottom of the film to prevent it from curling (Fig. 27).

12. With a wet, well squeezed out photographic viscose sponge (a soft sponge sold in photo supply stores) wipe both sides of the film *very gently* to remove excess water (Fig. 28). This will prevent water spots and hastens drying. The films should be left alone to dry, the windows must be closed and no one should move much in the room. Any draft or motion will stir up dust which may settle on the wet film and dry into the emulsion. Such dried in dust will cause a lot of trouble later on.

 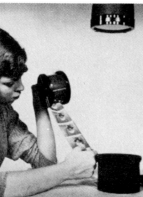  

17 Lift up end of roll with finger.   **18** Inspect emulsion side of film under safelight.   **19** Replace film on reel after inspection.   **20** Pour developer back into bottle.

21 Pour water into tank.   **22** Pour off water.   **23** Pour in hypo.   **24** Pour hypo back into its bottle.

25 Wash film in filtered running water.   **26** Agitate to remove air bubbles.   **27** Hang film up to dry.   **28** Wipe gently with viscose sponge.

13. Cut the dry film into convenient lengths (Fig. 29) and place the pieces individually into glassine envelopes (Fig. 30). Be careful and *always handle the film by the edges only.*

It makes no difference whether you develop rollfilm or cutfilm (or even glass plates), the procedure is the same. Do not neglect to agitate all films frequently throughout the process.

Judging Negative Density.

After some practice you will be able to judge film density under the safelight and stop development when the density of the negative is exactly right for print making. As a rule the best negative is the thinnest negative which will still produce a good quality print. A thin negative has less grain, shorter printing time and it is even somewhat sharper than the same negative developed to a higher density. For this reason make your negatives rather thin, but watch out for shadow details, do not lose them by making the negative too thin. In average work watch the shadow details when you develop by inspection, develop long enough to build up sufficient shadow detail. Disregard the highlights completely, proper exposure and your soft working developer will take care of them, they will not become too dense or blocked up.

When we say watch the shadow details we speak *only of those shadows which are to show detail in the print.* During development disregard those shadows in which no detail is desirable. Stop development when the rest of the negative has reached the proper density.

Exposure of the Negative.

We have no space in this book to present an adequate description of the exposure-development relationship in negative making. In fact, we plan a sequel to this book to be entitled "The Practical Way To Perfect Negatives" which will deal with this and many other aspects of negative making in full detail.

One of the principal advantages of development by inspection is that variations in exposure, deliberate or otherwise, are automatically taken care of because you see the condition of the negative and stop development at the proper time. The brief comment which follows is intended to clarify this point.

The most desirable exposure depends upon the contrast of the subject and the effect desired in the print. With a very flat subject, where an increase in contrast is wanted, expose for about one-half as long as indicated by the exposure meter. With the reduced exposure it will take longer for the negative to reach proper density and the prolonged development will result in increased contrast.

For subjects of average contrast give the indicated exposure.

For subjects of high contrast expose about three times as much as is indi-

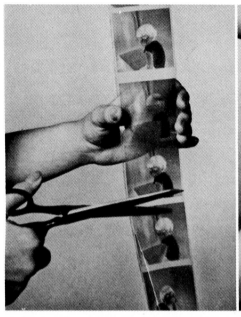 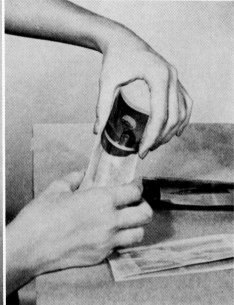

29 Cut film into convenient lengths. **30** Store film in glassine envelopes.

cated by the exposure meter and for subjects of very high contrast about six times as much. The increased exposure will bring about a shorter developing time which will produce a negative of reduced contrast, thus making up for the excessive contrast in the subject matter.

You should keep your exposures uniform if you use rollfilm. Stick to the exposures indicated by your exposure meter, or if you have to deviate from the meter indicated exposure to reduce subject contrast in the negative, use the whole roll for subjects of similar type and expose the whole roll with the same proportional increase* in exposure. This way your negatives will be evenly developed throughout the roll.

* or decrease

Examples.

As we mentioned above, after a little practice you will not have any difficulty determining proper negative density when you develop your films by inspection. Nevertheless, we would like to give you some idea of what a negative of proper density looks like. The negatives we show will give you only an indication of proper density because on the printed page the negative image will look somewhat different from the actual negative viewed by transmitted light. Your enlarger, its type and optical equipment also influence the negative density which will yield the best print using your equipment. But in spite of all these variables, the examples will start you off with some knowledge, will enable you to produce acceptable negatives, even when you develop your first films by inspection.

Fig. 31 shows the qualities desired in an average portrait. The negative with correct density is shown in Fig. 32. If the development is too short some details in the darker areas will be lost (Fig. 33). On the other hand, you should not wait until darkest area of the picture (hair) is full of detail on the negative, because meanwhile over-all negative density will become excessive. The details in the hair are not important enough here to sacrifice over-all negative quality (Fig. 34).

Fig. 35 is a picture with considerable contrast. Here shadow details are important parts of the composition, therefore the negative had to be developed until the shadows gained sufficient density (Fig. 36). In Fig. 37 shadow details appear, but not in sufficient density to produce the full shadow detail desired in the print. However, your desire for full shadow detail in the print should not carry you away and cause you to produce an altogether too dense negative (Fig. 38).

Fig. 39 is a picture with no shadow detail at all. When we developed the negative we disregarded the shadow areas, we just watched for sufficient highlight density (Fig. 40), and stopped development as soon as this had been obtained. Since the contrasty lighting produced very little exposure in the shadow areas these remain almost clear in the negative and readily produce a rich black in the print. If you develop a negative of this type do not make it too thin (Fig. 41), for too thin a negative will not yield a print with the desired dramatic low key effect. But do not try to get shadow detail in a negative which has none, because the lighting and exposure did not put them there. If you develop long enough to get density in such shadow areas, you will not have detail but fog, resulting from forced development. Meanwhile the important highlight areas will be badly blocked up (Fig. 42).

The examples above will help you to develop your negatives properly even if you are a beginner.

Summary.

Development by inspection has many advantages over the time and temperature method. Since you *see* what you are doing you cannot get anything but negatives with correct density. There will be no more too thin or too dense negatives for you. All your negatives will be approximately correct in density. The degree of exhaustion of the developer is of no great concern to you. In fresh developer your negatives will be developed faster, in old developer slower, but you just keep on developing until you get your negatives as dense as you want them to be. If your developer does not work for some reason (exhaustion, contamination, etc.) you can pour it off the film, fill the tank

31 Average portrait quality. **32** Negative with proper density. **33** Underdeveloped negative. **34** Overdeveloped negative.

35 Picture with considerable contrast. **36** Proper negative density. **37** Underdeveloped negative. **38** Overdeveloped negative.

  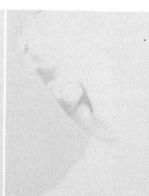 

39 Picture with no shadow detail. **40** Properly developed negative. **41** Underdeveloped negative. **42** Overdeveloped negative.

 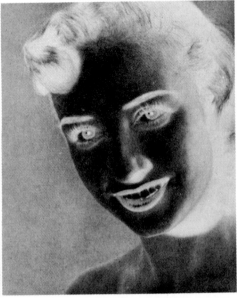

43 A very thin negative like this can be improved by intensification.

44 The same negative after intensification. It will now yield a much better print.

with water, mix a new batch of developer and continue developing with it. Only development by inspection gives you this safety, these consistently good results.

Negative Intensification and Reduction.

You may have negatives which are either too thin or too dense. You can intensify or reduce such negatives to improve their printing quality.

Negative intensification is simple. Buy a small tube of Victor's Intensifier (available in photo supply stores) and use it according to the instructions packed with it. Victor's Intensifier is very effective, cheap, and easy to use. Figs. 43 and 44 show a negative before and after intensification.

Negative reduction is used on negatives which are too dense. Before reduction you have to harden the negatives to counteract the emulsion softening effect of the reducers. Prepare the following hardener:

Negative Hardener

	Avoirdupois		Metric	
Water (about 125° F, 52° C)	24	ounces	750.0	cc
Formaldehyde (37 % solution by weight)*	1/3	ounce	11.0	cc
Sodium Carbonate (dessicated)	75	grains	5.5	grams
Add cold water to make	32	ounces	1.0	liter

*This is the concentration in which Formaldehyde is available commercially.

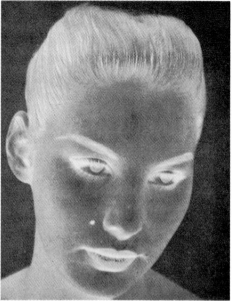

45 A dense, flat negative like this can be improved in the cutting reducer which reduces density and increases contrast.

46 The same negative after reduction in the cutting reducer. It will now yield a much better print.

Soak your negatives in water for about 10 minutes, then soak them in this hardener for about 3 minutes. Rinse the negatives after hardening, then immerse them in fresh acid fixing bath (your regular negative fixer) for five minutes. Wash negatives thoroughly before any further treatment.

You will use two kinds of reducers: the first is useful to treat negatives which are too dense over-all, it is called a "cutting reducer." You make it up in two solutions:

Cutting Reducer

	Avoirdupois	*Metric*
Solution A.:		
Water	1 oz.	30 cc
Potassium Ferricyanide	25 grains	2 grams
Solution B.:		
Water	1 quart	1 liter
Hypo crystals	2 oz.	60 grams

When the negative is ready for reduction (well washed, or presoaked for 10 minutes if it was dry) add Solution A to Solution B and immediately pour the mixture over the negative. Watch the negative closely while agitating it and when sufficient reduction has taken place remove it from the solution and wash it thoroughly before drying.

Once Solution A and B are mixed, the reducer spoils rapidly (in about 15 minutes) and therefore it should be used at once. Mix a fresh batch for every negative to be reduced. Fig. 45 shows a dense, flat negative, Fig. 46 is the same negative after reduction in the cutting reducer.

The second, so-called "super proportional" reducer, is used for negatives which are not only too dense, but also too contrasty. In other words, the highlight parts are too dense, but the shadow parts are just right, not too dense at all. To make such negatives printable you must reduce the overly dense highlight areas, while the shadow areas are changed very little, if at all. The super-proportional reducer will do just that.

Super-Proportional Reducer

Stock Solution

	Avoirdupois	Metric
Water (about 125° F, 52° C)	24 ounces	750.0 cc
Ammonium Persulfate	2 ounces	55.0 grams
Sulfuric Acid	¾ dram	3.0 cc
Cold water to make	32 ounces	1.0 liter

Handle the Sulfuric Acid with extreme care. It is a powerful chemical and can cause serious burns if it is allowed to reach any part of the body. Always add the acid to the water slowly and with constant stirring. Never add the water to the acid because the solution may boil and spatter the acid on the hands and face.

To make the Working Solution add 1 part of Stock Solution to 2 parts of water. Immerse the negative in the reducer (after 10 minutes presoaking in water, if dry) and watch the reduction carefully. When sufficient reduction has taken place rinse the negative and soak it in your regular negative fixer for about 5 minutes, then wash thoroughly before drying. Fig. 47 is too dense and contrasty. Fig. 48 is the same negative after it has been reduced in the super-proportional reducer.

If followed carefully, the above information on developing by inspection (combined with negative intensification and reduction to improve your existing negatives) will provide you with negatives which are easy to print.

More About Exposure.

And now, for a moment, we want to dwell upon the subject of exposure.

First of all, always use a photoelectric exposure meter. You can either measure the light reflected by the subject to the film, or the light falling on the subject. Either method is good but each requires a different technique.

The so-called *reflected light* meters (Weston, G. E., DeJur, etc.) measure the light reflected by the subject toward the camera. To measure only the light that counts (the picture producing light reflected by the subject) hold the meter close to the subject, pointed toward it. The meter is pointed at the most important part of the subject (toward the face, for example, in the case of a portrait).

47 This negative is too dense and too contrasty.

48 The super-proportional reducer improves such a negative by reducing both contrast and density.

You must be careful to read *only the light reflected by the subject*. This means that you must make sure that light from objects or sources outside of the important picture area does not reach the sensitive cell of the exposure meter. If light from the sky, a nearby light object, or from a light source (sun or photographic lights) is allowed to reach the meter, the reading will be upset and as a consequence the exposure will be inaccurate. It also may happen that a shadow is cast by your hand or the exposure meter itself on the area being read. This, of course, also upsets the correctness of the reading. Therefore you must be careful, we repeat, to read only the full light reflected by the subject. *The only way to do this is to examine carefully all light reaching the exposure meter during the reading, and hold the meter in such a way that all light is excluded except that reflected by the subject, while no shadow is being cast on the measured area.*

When you use an incident light meter (Norwood, etc.) you measure the light falling on the subject from the light source. The meter must be held in subject position pointed directly at the camera. The accuracy of the reading depends on how carefully the meter is pointed at the camera. A slight turning or tilting of the meter will change the exposure reading.

It happens sometimes that you cannot reach the subject to make your exposure meter reading from subject position. In such a case select a similar object nearby which has approximately the same light reflectance and receives the same lighting and take your exposure meter reading from that.

Before using an exposure meter, be sure that you are familiar with it. Study the instruction booklet supplied with your meter, carefully and thoroughly.

Equipment

How to Select an Enlarger?

Your major tool is the *enlarger*. It has to be good, though not necessarily expensive. Beginners often select an inadequate enlarger, because they don't know what they need and are sometimes misled by advertisements or salesmen anxious to make a sale. With the poorly selected enlarger they fail to get good results. They struggle for a while, then usually quit in disgust.

This need not happen to you. Select an enlarger with care, try it, test it before you finally decide to buy it. Reputable stores will allow you to try out all major pieces of equipment you buy. If you already have an enlarger and it does not give you good results, test it as if you were just going to buy it and, if it does not stand up under the tests, get rid of it, trade it in for a satisfactory enlarger. It is better to lose money on the trade in, than keep on struggling with it, wasting time, and money on materials, without being able to produce good results.

The price of the enlarger and its satisfactory working qualities are often not in proportion. There are cheap enlargers on the market which are entirely satisfactory, while some expensive ones are not so good. Fortunately it is easy to test an enlarger, you don't have to get stuck with a poor one, even if you are a beginner.

To give good service an enlarger should be rigid, aligned properly and in good optical and mechanical working order.

Testing Rigidity.

Rigidity is easily tested. First tighten all controls, as you would in getting ready to make an enlargement, then press down the baseboard with one hand and try to move the top of the upright post with the other (Fig. 49). It should feel solid, it should not wobble. Get hold of the post next and with the other hand try to move the head of the enlarger (Fig. 50). This, too, should feel solid, should not be loose. Finally hold the enlarger head and try to move the lensboard up and down, by grasping the lens, not by the focusing mechanism (Fig. 51). The lens board should not have play in it, either.

49 Testing the rigidity of the post. **50** Testing the rigidity of the head. **51** Testing the rigidity of the lensboard.

Testing the Alignment.

Proper alignment can be tested with a level, such as is sold in hardware stores. Level out the baseboard, make it horizontal and check it in both directions (length and width) with the level (Fig 52). If the baseboard is horizontal, the negative carrier and the lens should also be horizontal if the enlarger is aligned properly. Check both with the level (Fig. 53 and 54) in two directions (length and width). On enlargers which have a tilting device (for the whole head, negative carrier and/or lensboard) be sure that nothing is tilted, that all adjustments are in neutral position when you check alignment with the level.

If the negative carrier has no protruding part on which the level can be rested for the test, get a small sheet of glass (about 8x10″), insert it in place

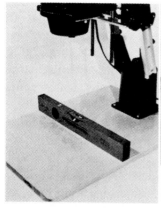  

52 Checking baseboard with level. **53** Checking negative carrier with level. **54** Checking lensboard with level.

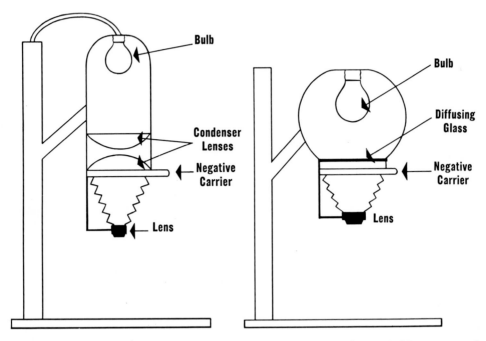

55 Cross section of typical condenser type of enlarger.

56 Cross section of typical diffusion type of enlarger.

of the negative carrier and rest the level on the protruding part of the glass.

For testing the alignment of the lens the top of the level is held against the lensboard or the bottom rim of the lens itself.

Types of Illumination.

The optical equipment of the enlarger consists of two parts: one directs the illumination, the other, the lens, projects the image. There are two types of enlarger systems in general use: the *condenser* type (Fig. 55) and the *diffusion* type (Fig. 56). The condenser type enlarger (Fig. 57) always has an incandescent bulb light source. The light passes through the condensers, which direct the light rays through the negative toward the lens and the enlarging paper. The condensers are big lenses made of clear glass, they resemble large magnifying glasses. Most enlargers have a set of two condenser lenses, some have one, others have three.

The condenser enlarger is fast (allows comparatively short exposure times), the enlargements it produces are crisp, have good contrast and reproduce the finest details in the negative.

The diffusion type enlarger (Fig. 58) has no condensers, it has a diffusing glass between light source and negative. The light source itself may be an incandescent bulb, fluorescent tubes or a so-called cold light. The diffusing glass is either a piece of ground glass or opal glass. The incandescent bulb and

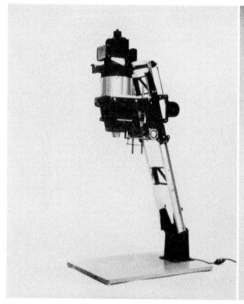

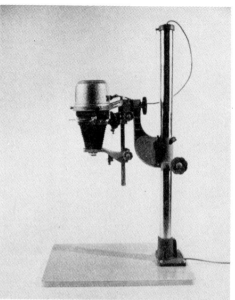

57 A condenser type of enlarger.　　　**58** A diffusion type of enlarger.

the fluorescent tubes do not vary in intensity, but the cold light sources do as they warm up and cool off. Therefore cold lights are practical only if the light source is kept turned on continuously and exposure is made either by a shutter in front of the lens or by taking off and replacing the lens cap. The diffused light enlargers are slower, require a longer exposure than would be needed to make a comparable print with a condenser enlarger. The prints are softer, less contrasty than prints made from the same negative with a condenser enlarger on the same paper. Diffused enlargers do not emphasize the finest details in the print as condenser enlargers do.

Which Type of Illumination Is Best?

One cannot say outright which is best, a condenser or a diffused type of enlarger. However, as a result of long experience, we can say this much: for small negatives, up to and including 2¼x3¼″ size, the condenser enlarger is better. For 35 mm negatives it is virtually indispensable. For larger negatives the choice depends on the kind of results you want to get: if you prefer crisp, lively prints with good contrast and critical detail, you should use a condenser enlarger. If you like soft prints, your choice will be a diffusion type enlarger. Because they do not emphasize the finest details, diffusing enlargers will minimize, on the print, the effects of grain, negative retouching and scratches. There are enlargers in which condenser and diffused light sources are readily

31

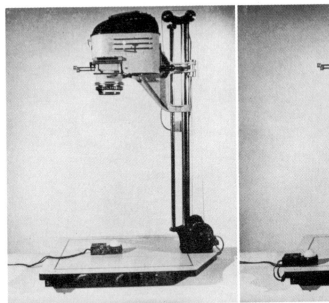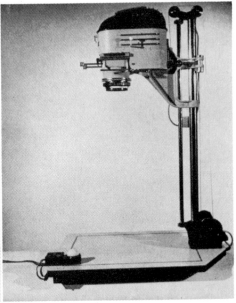

59 Light is measured at the center of the base-board.

60 Light is measured at the corner of the base-board.

interchangeable: with these you can use the light source best suited to the type of work being done.

Testing the Evenness of Light.

The illumination in the enlarger should be reasonably even over the entire surface of the negative. This is true for both condenser and diffusion types. You can check the evenness of illumination in a darkened room on a white paper placed on the enlarging easel: project a negative on the white paper, blow it up to about 11x14", make it sharp. Remove the negative. The light projected on the white paper in the easel should be even, there should be no "hot spot," the light should not be considerably stronger in the center than in the corners. You can check the evenness of light with your exposure meter: lay it down on the base board with the sensitive cell turned upward, toward the lens. Place it in the center (Fig. 59), note the light intensity indicated on the dial, then move the exposure meter into each of the four corners (Fig. 60). A *slight* falling off of the light in the corners does not matter, it occurs with even the better enlargers, but a considerable difference indicates that the light distribution of the enlarger is uneven, you should not buy such an enlarger. Before you make this test be sure that the enlarger is equipped with the light source (bulb) recommended for it by the manufacturer.

61
Focusing target used to test the lens of the enlarger.

The Lens.

If the best possible results are wanted the enlarger should be equipped with a lens designed for enlarging, not with a camera lens. It pays to buy a good lens with your enlarger, because only a good lens can turn a critically sharp negative into an equally sharp print. Also, the enlarger lens should be coated for better contrast and sharper detail. The quality of the enlarger lens is not always in proportion with its price. Some reasonably priced lenses are quite satisfactory.

Testing the Lens.

You can be sure of the working quality of an enlarging lens only after you have tested it. It is simple to make a practical test: Buy a so-called "focusing target" in your camera store. This is a piece of film on which simple designs appear in very fine line and high contrast (Fig. 61). The focusing target is available in all standard negative sizes, get one the same size as your negatives. Place the focusing target in the negative carrier and project its image on the white paper in the easel. Move the enlarger high on its post to get a considerable degree of enlargement. Focus until the center of the focusing target is sharp on the easel. Now the entire image of the focusing target should be sharp, from corner to corner. If you cannot make any part of the focusing target critically sharp on the easel, or if the center is sharp but the edges are not (or vice versa), your enlarger lens is not satisfactory. Exchange it for one

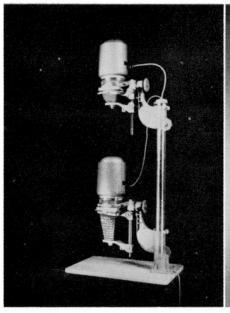 

62 The enlarger head moves up and down on the post.

63 The lens can be moved up and down for focusing.

which will stand the described test. However, be sure that your enlarger is properly aligned (negative carrier, lens and baseboard are parallel) before you pass judgment on the performance of your lens. Improper alignment will prevent the lens from projecting a sharp image of the focusing target from corner to corner. Check proper alignment with the use of a level, as described above.

The *speed* (largest opening) of the enlarger lens is not too important. The average enlarger lens has an f:4.5 or f:6.3 opening.

The *focal length* of the enlarger lens should approximately match the diagonal (distance between two opposite corners) of the negative which is being enlarged.

Checking the Mechanical Working Order of the Enlarger.

Next you have to check the mechanical working order of your enlarger. This, too, is simple. There are two mechanical functions your enlarger has to perform satisfactorily: the whole head has to move up and down on the post (Fig. 62) to control the degree of enlargement and the lens has to move up and down for focusing (Fig. 63). Both movements must be smooth working. You should be able to lock the enlarger head on the post in any position. The up and down focusing movement of the lens should not be loose, the lens must stay put in any position without slipping or backlash.

Other Features.

While most enlargers are to be focused manually, there are also enlargers with automatic focus. The autofocus enlargers (as they are called) are very helpful in mass production work, but for our purpose, the making of top quality enlargements, they are not necessary. The enlarging ratio (degree of enlargement) of autofocus enlargers is limited and they can get out of focus, too.

Negative Carriers.

Some enlargers are equipped with a glassless (sometimes called dustless) negative carrier, others with one using two sheets of glass for holding the negative.

Glassless negative carriers are more popular, you only need to clean the negative to avoid spots on the print. If the negative carrier has glasses in it, you have to clean them, too. Glasses, however, keep the negative absolutely flat, which cannot be said of the glassless negative carriers.

Whatever the theoretical advantages and disadvantages may be, in practical work both types give satisfactory service.

Negative Sizes Accommodated by an Enlarger.

Enlargers are made to accomodate a certain negative size. This actually refers to the largest negative which can be "blown up" using that enlarger. Negatives smaller than the designated size can also be enlarged with any enlarger simply by using another negative carrier with a smaller opening to hold the smaller negative. With the glass type negative carriers it is sufficient to place a black paper mask between the glasses to cover up the superfluous area around the smaller negative.

There is one drawback when you enlarge a negative smaller than that for which the enlarger was made: the size of the largest print which you can project on the baseboard will also become smaller, thus limiting the size of the enlargements you can make conveniently. This drawback is eliminated if you change the lens of the enlarger to another of shorter focal length, to approximately match the diameter of the smaller negative being enlarged.

On the diffusion type enlargers you can change the lens to another one of a different focal length without any ill effect. With condenser type enlargers, however, the condenser must also be changed if the lens is changed, otherwise loss of light and possibly uneven illumination may result. Each lens of a different focal length has a matching set of condensers to be used with it. Some enlargers come with interchangeable matching sets of lenses, condensers and negative carriers which enables their user to enlarge efficiently several different negative sizes. The Omega DII, for example, has matched sets for several sizes, from 4x5" down to 35 mm negatives.

Other Items You Need.

Other items you need for enlarging are: easel, safelight, trays, tongs, thermometer, graduate and timer.

The Easel.

To get accurately measured straight margins around your prints you have to have a good easel. They are not cheap. If in the beginning you do not want to spend the amount needed for a good easel, don't buy any. Just tape the enlarging paper by the corners to the baseboard of the enlarger. This will not hinder you in making fine enlargements, but will save you the trouble and aggravation which a cheap easel would cause.

The Safelight.

The safelight should be a good one, also. Get one in which the safety filters can be changed (Kodak makes several good safelights). For most of your work you will use a Wratten OA or similar yellowish green safelight filter which supplies sufficient light for you to see by during enlarging. The safelight should be equipped with a regular 10 Watt bulb. Do not use a larger bulb, it may fog your enlarging paper and overheat the safelight, causing damage to the safety filter.

The Trays.

You need four trays: one for developer, one for shortstop, one for hypo and one to wash your prints in. The size of the trays depends on the size of the largest prints you intend to make. If you make 8x10" and smaller prints most of the time, you should buy 3—8x10" trays and 1—11x14". It does not pay to get trays larger than you need, because they only take up more room in storage and more chemicals to fill them. If you are a beginner, or nearly so, get three 8x10" and one 11x14" tray. When you want to make larger prints you can always buy the larger trays, but even then it will be better to use the small trays when you make smaller prints. Enamel trays are the most common. They chip rather easily, unless you are extra careful (and most of us are not). Hard rubber or stainless steel trays are more expensive to buy, but they are cheaper in the long run because they practically never need replacement (especially the stainless steel).

Small Items.

You need two pairs of tongs for handling prints in the solutions. They are made of plastic or stainless steel. Both are good. The two pairs you buy should be different, so that one can be readily distinguished from the other under the safelight.

The thermometer should be the type which can be clipped on to the edge of the tray.

Get a quart size glass graduate.

The Timer.

For enlarging you *must have an audible timer*. You cannot look at a clock during enlarging, you must look at what you are doing. You cannot get good results if you have to keep on looking at the timer to see when the exposure time is up.

Probably on account of the unfamiliarity of the timer manufacturers with the process of making fine enlargements, even most of the expensive "automatic" timers are silent. The automatic feature, which shuts off the enlarger at the end of a preset period, is useless when you do fine enlarging, because you have to time accurately, not only the full exposure, but also the duration of different manipulations *during* exposure, for which the automatic timer has no provision. The only solution is the use of an audible timer, which enables you to time the exposure or any part of it accurately, simply by counting the ticks of the timer. Any loud ticking alarm clock will serve as an audible timer, after you have learned to count the ticks without getting confused. The only audible photographic timer is made by General Electric. It gives a loud tick every second, making it easy for you to time your exposure. It has the automatic feature, too, turning off your enlarger after a preset time. The automatic feature can be made inoperative and the timer can be set to just indicate time by clicking off the seconds.

Buy good enlarging equipment. It will be cheaper in the long run, because good equipment will give you trouble free service for a long time. Besides, it will enable you to do good work right from the beginning. However, good equipment does not necessarily mean expensive equipment. With wise shopping and perhaps buying second hand items in good condition, you can acquire all you need for a rather modest amount.

Enlarging Papers

Many excellent workers will advise you to use one or another of the papers on the market as the "best" for making fine prints. The fact is that all papers on the market are good, they will produce excellent prints, if you know how to make such prints.

Paper Classifications.

The available papers belong to several classes with different character-istics and for good results you must select the proper kind for each print you make. Many of us do not make the right selection and when we get unsatis-factory results we blame the paper, saying that it is "bad," instead of blaming our poor judgment in selecting the paper.

Basically there are two groups of papers: the cold tone and the warm tone papers. The cold tone papers produce pictures with rich blacks and pure gray tones, prints made on warm tone papers have warm brownish or greenish-brown tones.

The so-called bromide (Ansco Brovira, etc.) and fast chlorobromide papers (Kodabromide, Velour Black, Varigam, etc.) are cold tone papers, the slow chlorobromides (Ansco Indiatone, DuPont Warmtone, Kodak Opal, etc.) and chlorides are warm tone papers. Also, there is an intermediate group, the medium speed chlorobromide papers (Ansco Cykora, Kodak Platino and Medalist, etc.), which have tones warmer than those of the cold tone papers, but not as warm as the tones of the warm tone papers.

The words: bromide, chlorobromide and chloride refer to the silver salts used in making the light sensitive gelatin emulsion of the enlarging papers.

There are three major manufacturers of photographic papers in the United States: Ansco, DuPont and Kodak. All three makes are good, but they have slightly different characteristics in each class, which points to the reason for one of the most important rules of successful enlarging: *select one kind and make of paper and stick to it.* After a little practice you will become familiar with that paper and will be able to get consistently good results with it. If, on the other hand, you keep changing papers, you will not be able to get such consistently good results. If you want to use two or all three types of papers you may choose one type made by one manufacturer and another type made by another manufacturer. This is O.K., as long as you stick to your selected paper in each class, regardless of the results you get in the beginning. You can be sure that the paper you are using is good and the fault is with you if you do not get the desired results. So do not change the make of paper you use, hoping you will get better results with another paper. You won't. Just follow our instructions and you will get good results on any paper you may select.

What we have said above is valid for the papers made by the three big companies: Ansco, DuPont and Kodak. Other domestic makes and imported papers are also available. Some of these are excellent, others not so good. You should use them only if you are an expert printer and able to judge the results for yourself when you evaluate the merits of each paper. But even if you are an expert you will settle down in the long run to the use of papers made by the big three for most of your work.

Surface, Contrast and Color of Paper.

Beside the tones they produce photographic papers have three more inherent characteristics: surface, contrast and color of base. There is a variety of paper surfaces; glossy, semi-glossy, matte, smooth, rough, etc. The selection of surface is up to you, it is mostly a matter of taste, but you should familiarize yourself with what is available to be able to make the proper selection. Prints made for reproduction, for example, should be printed on glossy paper. The glossy paper is also best for pictures in which the showing of fine detail is important. Semi-glossy and semi-matte, smooth or fine grained papers are suitable for a great number of pictures. Matte and rough surfaces have a limited use in certain portrait and pictorial work.

The contrast of photographic papers is inherent in the emulsion. Most papers come in several contrast grades. For each negative you will have to find the paper with the right inherent contrast to produce a print of proper contrast. This is not difficult. Specific instructions are given in the chapter on print contrast.

Some papers are made in one contrast grade only. Negatives of proper matching contrast can be printed on these. The contrast of one paper, DuPont's "Varigam," can be controlled over a wide range by using special filters in front of the lens of the enlarger.*

The paper stock used to make enlarging papers is either white, off white, cream or buff in color. The first three are most popular, buff papers are used less frequently.

Papers, like other sensitized photo materials, are dated. The expiration date appears on every package. Always use fresh, "in date," papers.

If you are a beginner start with four packages of 8x10″ paper, like Velour Black or Kodabromide #1, #2, #3 and #4, for example.

*For complete instructions on "Varigam" read PRINTING WITH "VARIGAM," Camera Craft, $1.95.

Chemicals

You need three solutions to start enlarging: developer, shortstop and hypo. The exposed enlarging paper shows no image, the developer turns the latent invisible image into a visible one. The shortstop stops the action of the developer by neutralizing its chemical effect. The hypo makes the image permanent by removing from the emulsion all unexposed light sensitive silver compounds which were left there after development.

Basically there are two types of developers: a normal working and a soft working type. Kodak Dektol, Ansco Vividol and DuPont 53-D are normal developers; Kodak Selectol, Ansco Ardol and DuPont 51-D, for example, are soft working developers. There are other good developers made by independent manufacturers, like Edwal, FR, etc. Each manufacturer recommends his own formulas for his papers, but actually there is not much difference between the various makes, you can use the developer of one manufacturer to develop papers made by another.

Stick to one developer and use it for most of your work. That way you will know exactly what the developer does and will get good results consistently. On rare occasions you will need a special developer to get a certain effect in a print, but this will seldom happen.

Always use prepared developers. They are inexpensive, easy to use and will save you a lot of trouble. Those "secret" formulas which some experts will advise you to make up and use, usually aren't any better than developers made by reputable manufacturers.

Stock solutions of the developers can be stored in a tightly stoppered brown bottle for a considerable time (for months) without appreciable change in their working efficiency. Full bottles of the solutions keep better than half filled ones.

The shortstop is diluted Acetic Acid. Use 28% Acetic Acid* as your shortstop *stock solution.*

There are two kinds of hypo in general use: one with, the other without hardener. For average use the ready made hypo with hardener is advisable, but if you want to give your prints after treatments, like toning, over-all or

---

*To make 28% acetic acid from glacial acetic acid dilute 3 parts of glacial acetic acid with 8 parts of water.

local reduction, intensification, etc., then you should make your own hypo without hardener:

Non-Hardening Fixing Bath

	Avoirdupois	*Metric*
Water (about 125° F, 52° C)	24 ounces	750.0 cc
Sodium Thiosulfate (Hypo)	10 ounces	250.0 grams

When thoroughly dissolved, add:

	Avoirdupois	*Metric*
Potassium Metabisulfite	1 ounce	25.0 grams
Cold water to make	32 ounces	1.0 liter

To make your working solutions from prepared chemicals follow the instructions printed on the containers in which you buy them.

Setting Up for Work

And now we come to the point where you have all your equipment and materials and are ready to start enlarging. You may have a darkroom or you may use the kitchen or the bathroom for that purpose. The looks and the layout of your darkroom have nothing to do with the quality of the work you will do in it. It is important to understand this because many of us feel that we cannot make top quality enlargements unless we have an "adequate" darkroom. The truth is that you can make fine enlargements in the oddest, least convenient emergency darkroom *if you know how*. In other words, you must learn enlarging. When you know how to make good enlargements you will be able to make them anywhere, regardless of the dark space you have to do it in.

Darkroom Must Be Dark.

The only strict requirement for a suitable darkroom is that it *must be dark*. You cannot work in a darkroom which leaks light. If you have trouble making the space you want to use as a darkroom completely dark, then work at night. Almost any space you may want to use will be sufficiently dark at night, even without special efforts to make it so. But whether you work during the day or at night, you must be sure that your darkroom is dark.

Basic Setup.

In the darkroom you should have space for the enlarger and the three processing trays. These can be cramped into a rather small area, therefore many people are able to use a closet to work in. Of course, we are not saying that you should have a small or inconvenient darkroom, but we want to point out that you can do enlarging almost anywhere: in a small apartment, in a furnished room or even in a tent. However, if you have the space, the means and the desire, fix up a "dream darkroom," it is always pleasant to have a convenient place to work. But regardless of how fancy or how modest your darkroom is, you must have the basic setup shown in Fig. 64.

Place the three trays next to each other. Hang up the safelight over the trays, at least three feet away from them. On the other side of the darkroom set up the enlarger. This is the simplest and most convenient setup. The

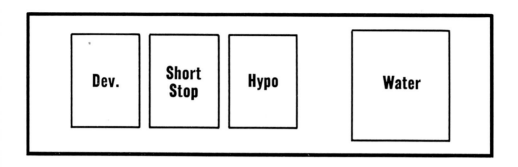

BASIC SETUP
OF DARKROOM

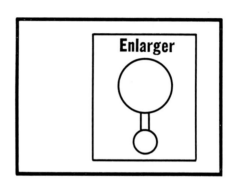

64 Basic darkroom setup.

enlarger and the trays should not be placed side by side because the accidental splashing of solutions will soil the enlarger, the easel and the enlarging paper. Accordingly the basic setup should consist of one dry and one wet working surface, separated from each other. The audible timer can be placed at any convenient spot. One pair of tongs is at the developer tray, the other pair is next to the hypo tray. It is a good idea to place several layers of newspaper under the trays. These can be discarded after use, will help keep the darkroom clean and will also reduce the work of cleaning up after each working session.

If you work in the kitchen or bathroom you have running water at hand. Place a somewhat larger tray in the sink or bathtub for washing the prints. A few clothespins attached to the sides of the tray will prevent the prints from being carried over the edge by the overflowing water. If you have no running water where you work just keep a trayful of water handy. Keep another tray in the bathtub or kitchen sink and transfer the prints from your water tray into it every once in a while.

Pour the hypo into the hypo tray. If you use prepared hypo follow the instructions on the can or bottle for dissolving or diluting it. If you make your own without hardener according to the previously mentioned formula, use the hypo without dilution.

When you are finished for the day, pour the hype back into its bottle. It can be reused. Before each enlarging session test the working strength of your hypo with a hypo testing solution (Hypo Check, Hyp-a-test, etc.). Add one drop of the testing solution to the hypo. If nothing happens the hypo is good, if a yellowish cloud develops where the drop hit the hypo, then the hypo is exhausted, should be replaced with fresh solution.

Prepare the shortstop by adding 2 oz. of 28% acetic acid to a quart of water.

Finally make the developer working solution according to the instructions supplied with the developer you use. We use Kodak's Dektol for most of our work, one part stock solution diluted with two parts of water.

The working solution must be discarded after each working session. Mix a fresh batch every time you start to make enlargements.

Fill the trays about half way with the solutions.

Testing the Darkness of your Darkroom.

The first thing you have to do is to make a darkness test. Take a small piece of enlarging paper and lay it down next to the developer tray. The paper should lay with the emulsion side up. With most papers you can identify the emulsion side easily enough: it is the shiny side or the one having the texture. If there is a slight curl in the paper it will be toward the emulsion side. With smooth matte papers it may take a little practice to tell the two sides apart.

Place a coin on the paper and let it stand there for four minutes (Fig. 65). At the end of the four minutes develop the paper for three minutes, then rinse it in the shortstop and drop it in the hypo tray. Turn on the roomlight (regular white room illumination) and examine the test piece. It should be clear, no trace of the coin should show. If the place where the coin covered the paper is marked by a disc of a lighter shade, however slight, it means that the darkroom is not safe to work in (Fig. 66). Examine it for light leaks. If there are no light leaks, then probably the safelight is the culprit. Place it farther away from the trays and be sure that you have the proper size bulb in it (10 Watts for most safelights). Continue making darkness tests until your test indicates that your darkroom is safe, until no trace of the coin will show on the paper. For this test always use the fastest paper you are going to use. If you use both fast and slow chlorobromide papers, for example, use the fast paper for the test.

How to Use the Enlarger.

Before you start to work learn to operate your enlarger. It is simple, nevertheless you have to learn it. *Read the instruction book* supplied with

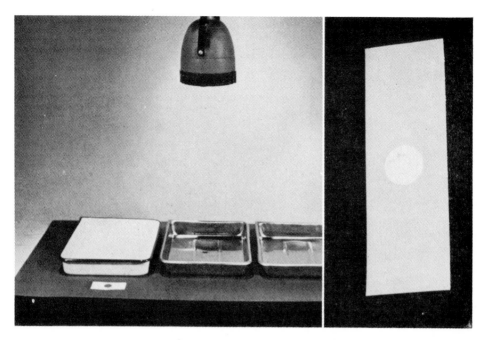

65 Testing light tightness of darkroom and safety of safelight.

66 This result indicates that darkroom is not light tight or safelight is too strong or too close to work.

your enlarger. If there is none, ask the clerk in the store where you bought it to explain the features of your enlarger or, perhaps, ask its previous owner if you bought the enlarger from a private party.

Cleaning the Enlarger.

Be sure that the enlarger is *clean*. Clean the lens on both sides *gently*. First brush it off with a soft camel's hair brush, then breathe on it and wipe it (gently) with a soft piece of clean chamois leather or lens tissue.

The condensers, too, must be cleaned. Usually there are two condensing lenses and you must clean each of them on both sides. On a diffusion type enlarger the diffusing glass must be cleaned. On some enlargers you have to dismantle the condensing unit in order to be able to clean the curved inside surfaces of the condensers. Do it once when you get the enlarger, after that you only have to do it about three or four times a year, more often if your place of work is dusty and/or humid.

If there are glasses in your negative carrier to hold the film flat you must clean them gently every time you start enlarging (but not every time you put a negative in the carrier).

Always keep a dust cover on your enlarger when it is not in use. If your

45

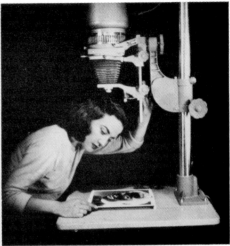

67 Most enlarger lenses have an adjustable diaphragm.   **68** Enlarger being focused.

enlarger is the folding (store-away) type, keep it in its carrying case.

When your enlarger is clean place the negative in the negative carrier, emulsion side down. The dull emulsion side should face the lens, the shiny back side faces the light source. Just before you place the negative carrier back into the enlarger blow on one side of the negative and brush it gently but thoroughly with a flat, soft camel's hair brush (about 1" wide) *while you blow*. Brushing loosens up the dust particles, blowing carries them away. Repeat it on the other side of the negative. Be sure that you blow dry, so that no droplets of saliva will settle on the negative. If your negative carrier has glasses, repeat the "blowing and brushing" procedure on both sides of each of the glasses. This simple procedure is extremely important because it removes most of the dust and lint particles from the negative (and glasses) which later would cause unsightly spots on the enlargements and a lot of spotting work. Be sure to handle the negative (and the glasses too, if you have them) only *by the edges*. Never lay a finger on either side of the negative or of the glasses.

Focusing.

Now, that the cleaned negative is in the clean enlarger, the next step is to focus. Turn on the light in the enlarger, turn off the roomlight (not the safelight). Place a white sheet of paper in the easel (ordinary paper for focusing, *not* enlarging paper). The lens opening of the enlarger can be adjusted with a diaphragm (Fig. 67) just like the lens of your camera. Open up the diaphragm fully. You see the negative image projected on the easel. Turn the focusing knob of the enlarger, first one way, then the other way, (Fig. 68),

69 Inaccurate focusing results in a blurred picture.

70 Careful focusing results in a sharp picture.

until the image becomes as sharp as you can make it (Fig. 69 and 70). If you have trouble with seeing the projected image use a focusing aid called Focus-Aid, made by Fedco and sold in photo supply stores. It is good and makes focusing easier. Most of us, however, do not need the focusing aid.

When the projected image is sharp see if the image size on the easel is what you want it to be. If it is too small raise the enlarger, if it is too large, lower it. Move the easel until you get projected on it that part of the negative which is to be included in the print, arranged the way you want it. This is called *cropping* or making the *composition,* of which we speak later.

Whenever you raise or lower the enlarger you will have to focus again.

Stopping Down the Lens.

You should stop down the lens to about f:8 when you have the enlarger at the proper height and the projected image is sharp. The f: stop markings are engraved around the ring with which you set the diaphragm opening. The f:8 opening is good for average use, change it if the exposure time for a particular negative and paper combination turns out to be too short to manage. The average exposure time should be about 10 seconds or more. A very short exposure does not give you a chance to repeat it accurately, if necessary, or to do any manipulating. Accordingly, stop down the lens of the enlarger to an opening where the exposure will be in the neighborhood of 10 seconds. If the exposure becomes unreasonably long (running into minutes), open up the lens of the enlarger to shorten the exposure, but always leave it stopped down to the next to the largest opening. This will correct any small error you may have made in focusing or unevenness of focus caused by a slight curving of the negative in the negative carrier. This latter condition frequently occurs with glassless negative carriers. Thus if you have an f:4.5 lens, stop down

47

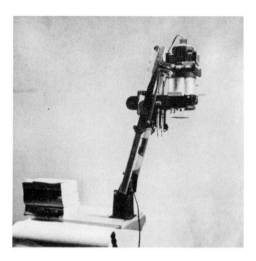

to at least f:5.6 after focusing. In actual work you will find that you will most frequently use f:8, f:11 or f:16 lens openings.

When the negative is projected on the easel, cropping is as you want it and after careful focusing the lens is stopped down, you are ready to make your first print. But before we get to that you should learn how to handle the enlarger when you want to make extra large or extra small prints, or if you want to correct linear distortion in the picture.

Making Extra Large Prints.

When you have raised the enlarger as high as it will go on its post you get the largest image that the enlarger can ordinarily produce. If you want to make your print still larger you have to do one of two things: you either will have to turn around the enlarger and project the image off the baseboard (on the floor) or you have to tilt it to a horizontal position and project the image on the wall.

On most enlargers you can swing the head around the post of the enlarger 180 degrees. When you do it you have to place a heavy weight on the baseboard, or clamp the baseboard to the table on which it stands, otherwise the enlarger will topple over and may be damaged (Fig. 71). The making of an extra large print requires the same technique as an ordinary size print.

Some enlarger heads can be tilted to project horizontally. When the head is tilted to an *exactly* horizontal position (Fig. 72) then the projected image will fall on the wall of the darkroom. The enlarging paper of the desired size can be taped on the wall and the enlargement thus made. The size of the enlargement can be controlled by changing the distance between enlarger and wall. The negative must be exactly parallel to the wall, otherwise distortion will result.

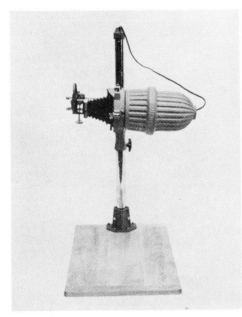

72 The head of the enlarger is tilted to a horizontal position for projection on wall.

73 Focus by moving the enlarger head when making very small prints.

Making Very Small Prints.

When the enlarger is placed in its lowest position on the post and the projected image is made sharp you have the smallest image you can ordinarily get. Sometimes, however, you may want to make an even smaller print, perhaps a tiny reduction.

To make the smallest print your enlarger can produce proceed in this way: raise the enlarger head quite high on the post and lower the lens as far as it will go with the focusing mechanism (increase the distance between lens and film as much as possible). Prop up the easel with a few thick books or other suitable objects, raise it about 6 inches above the baseboard if your enlarger is small, about 10 inches if it is large. Turn on the enlarger and focus it *by lowering the enlarger head on its post, without moving the focusing mechanism from its lowest position.* Move the enlarger head slowly until the projected image is sharp (Fig. 73). This image is the smallest picture you can make with your enlarger. To make it slightly larger: raise the lens a *little* with the focusing mechanism and make the image sharp again by moving the head of the enlarger. Repeat the procedure if you want to make the print still larger.

To make even smaller prints you have to use an auxiliary lens (Portra +3, a so-called camera portrait attachment) over the lens of the enlarger, or

74 Linear distortion caused by tilting the cam-   **75** . . corrected during enlarging.
era upward . . .

you have to change the lens of the enlarger to one of a shorter focal length. Use the technique just described to adjust sharpness and image size with the lens plus auxiliary lens combination or with the lens of shorter focal length. Use a very small lens opening when you make reductions (about f:22 or smaller).

Correcting Distortion.

Sometimes you have to print negatives in which the subject shows linear distortion. This happens mostly when the picture was taken with a tilted camera. A typical example of this is a scene in which the tops of buildings seem to run together (Fig. 74). Such distortion can be corrected—lines which run together can be made parallel again during enlarging (Fig. 75). On enlargers with a tilting head all you have to do is to tilt the head until the lines in the projected image become parallel (Fig. 76). Tilt the enlarger so that the top of the projected image, where the lines run together, is farther away from the enlarger head (lens) than the bottom portion of the image where the lines are the farthest apart. When you tilt the enlarger the image will move, you have to move the easel with it.

The other method of correcting distortion is to leave the enlarger alone and tilt the easel. The end of the easel where the distorted lines are farthest

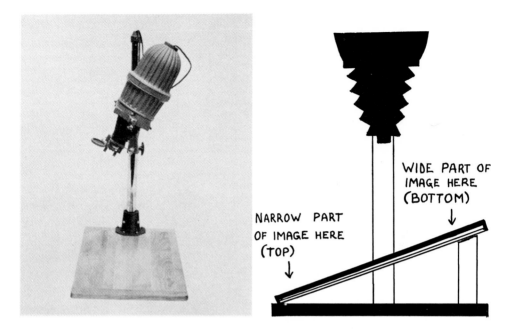

NARROW PART OF IMAGE HERE (TOP) ↓

WIDE PART OF IMAGE HERE (BOTTOM) ↓

76 Head of enlarger is tilted to correct linear distortion.

77 Easel is tilted to correct linear distortion.

apart should be raised until the lines become parallel on the projected image (Fig. 77).

Whichever method you use you will find that you cannot make the entire projected image sharp with the lens wide open. When one end is sharp the other is out of focus and vice versa. Make the image sharp at the center and stop down the enlarger lens until you get the entire image into focus. The more the enlarger or easel is tilted the more you have to stop down to get the entire image sharp.

Some enlargers have a tilting negative carrier and/or lensboard to help you correct linear distortion. Instruction booklets supplied with such enlargers explain those features.

Composition

What Is Composition?

Enlarging consists of two phases: 1. The *creative* phase, when you decide what your print should look like, and 2. The *technical* phase, when you actually make the print. *Composition* is part of the creative phase. It is the act of selecting and arranging in the print the various elements of the subject present in the negative. The negative is just the starting point. When you make your enlargement you have to decide how much of the subject should be included in it and how it should be arranged within the picture area for best results. The act of composing during the enlarging process is often called *cropping*.

Please Yourself.

When composing your picture remember one thing: *nobody* has ever made a picture that pleased *everybody*. No matter what composition you select, there will be people who won't like it, who will tell you that another composition would be better. The question arises: Whom shall you please with your pictures? How can you anticipate the reaction of your audience to any one picture, to any one composition? The answer is simple and convenient: *Do not try to please anybody but yourself.*

At the time you took the picture some quality in the subject matter appealed to you. In your mind you had a more or less clear idea of what the finished picture would look like. Many of the factors which determine composition are, of course, fixed at the time the negative is exposed, but there is still a great opportunity to improve the picture compositionally during the enlarging process.

But how does one decide what to do to arrive at the "best" composition? The essential thing is that you remember that quality in the subject matter which originally appealed to you and then do everything that you can to bring out that quality in the picture as forcefully as possible. This is the way most experienced photographers make their pictures.

Guides to Composition in Enlarging.

We fully realize that the above statement is not very helpful to the be-

78 (Upper left) L-shaped cardboards used to find pleasing compositions. **79** (Upper right) Print from entire negative. **80** (Lower left) The L's in use. **81** (Lower right) Final print arrived at by using the L's.

ginner. Such a person needs more specific advice to help him get started and to keep him going until he gains experience. For this purpose we describe composition in enlarging as it is distilled from our own experience, emphasizing that the guides we present are not the "rules" or "laws" of composition as they are generally known. Nevertheless, you will find them helpful, probably because the description is short and because it avoids the lengthy theoretical discussions and controversies usually entered into on the subject of composition.

Below you find our own condensation of the most essential factors which apply to composition during the enlarging process.

To compose your enlargements you must take two steps for each print you make:

1. Eliminate.   2. Arrange.

82 Print from entire negative.

83 A better picture is found in a small portion of the negative.

1. Eliminate.

Make simple compositions. *Eliminate unessential details.* If effective composition could be expressed in one word that word would be: *simplicity*. The simpler you can make your composition the better your picture will be. When you make your enlargement aim to include only those objects, or those parts of an object, which will make the most effective picture as you see it. Eliminate everything else. If you are in doubt whether or not a certain part is necessary, eliminate it mercilessly. The average photographer tends to include too much in every enlargement.

There is a simple aid which can help you to discover a good composition for each negative you enlarge, it is a pair of "L" shaped cardboards, such as are shown in Fig. 78. Make a contact print or an enlargement of the entire negative. Such a print is shown in Fig. 79. Lay the "L" shaped cardboards on your print so that they form a frame (Fig. 80). Move the "L's" over the picture, open and close them until the framed portion appears to be a pleasing picture. Use this composition to make your final print of that negative (Fig. 81).

Fig. 82 is another print from the entire negative. While the subject is rather interesting, the print is not. A better, more interesting print was made by eliminating most of the negative, enlarging a comparatively small portion of it (Fig. 83).

Fig. 84 contains the full negative and it makes a rather striking picture.

84 Print from entire negative.

85 Definite improvement is brought about by cropping.

However, the feature of this photograph is the opening in the wall through which distant buildings can be seen. This part is rather small in the print. If we make the image larger and eliminate part of it, we obtain a better balanced, more interesting composition (Fig. 85).

The elimination of a small part of the negative is often sufficient to get an improved picture. Fig. 86 is a good picture as it is, but the pose of the fawn,

86 Print from entire negative.

87 Cropping just a little from both sides improves the picture.

89 Print from entire negative improved by . . .   **90** . . . placing important elements in strong position in picture space.

while natural, seems to be somewhat awkward. Cropping just a little from both sides results in a better composition (Fig. 87).

Cropping will improve about 95% of the pictures you make, but there are occasions when it is best to print from the entire negative. Fig. 88 is an example. Eliminating any part of this image would make it less, rather than more interesting.

Figs. 89 to 98 are additional examples to show you how better, more striking compositions were achieved by eliminating unessential parts of pictures.

91 Print from entire negative improved by . . .   **92** . . . eliminating uninteresting foreground.

88 Print from entire negative. Cropping this picture would make it less, rather than more interesting.

93 Print from entire negative improved by . . .   **94** . . . cropping which makes the boat seem larger and more important.

95 Print from entire negative improved by . . .   **96** . . . cropping which gives us a closer look at these faces.

97 Print from entire negative improved by . . .

98 . . . cropping which eliminates distracting details.

2. Arrange.

Arrange within the picture area the parts which remain after having selected the essential and having eliminated the unessential details. Arranging the subject within the picture area is an important step. There are many arrangements possible for each subject. The selection of the best one is up to you, but as a guide we can mention that you often get an effective arrangement if the most important part (center of interest) of your enlargement is placed off center, in the direction of any of the four corners, but not too close to the corner. Also, ask yourself these questions before you decide the final arrangement for each enlargement you make:

Will tilting make this a better picture?

Should the main subject be placed high or low within the picture area?

Should the main subject be placed nearer to either side?

Would reversing the image improve the picture?

Fig. 99 shows a rather unusual subject. In reality the trapeze was hanging without motion. Yet, we wanted to give the impression that the trapeze was in motion. The desired effect was achieved by tilting the image (Fig. 100), by turning the easel under the enlarger.

Placing the subject high in the picture made Fig. 101 more provocative.

99 Straight print.

100 Tilting the subject in the picture space creates an illusion of motion, the trapeze appears to be swinging.

101
Placing the head high in the picture space enhances the provocative pose and expression.

102 A pleasing composition was made by placing the subject well to the side, with the window acting as a balancing element.

Some pictures can be improved by placing the subject low.

A pleasing composition was made in Fig. 102 by placing the subject well to the side, with the window acting as a balancing element.

Consider Other Possibilities.

Explore your negatives. Sometimes a negative will yield several different, equally good compositions.

Fig. 103 is a full print from the entire negative, not a bad picture as it is. In Fig. 104 the row of boats was made into a tight horizontal composition. For Fig. 105 the large group of boats was enlarged to fill the picture. Finally in Fig. 106 the boats were placed high in the picture space and an expanse of water in the foreground was made part of the composition. All these from one negative.

Fig. 107 is a full print of a portrait negative. Figs. 108, 109 and 110 are all good, but different prints made from that negative.

Some subjects are naturally divided, two entirely different pictures can be made from such negatives. Fig. 111, for example, shows a portion of a door with a figure in relief next to a panel of glass, in which an interesting

103, 104, 105, 106

Several good but slightly different compositions may be obtained from a single negative. Print from entire negative is seen in upper left.

107, 108, 109, 110

Several good but slightly different compositions may be obtained from a single portrait negative. Print from entire negative is seen in upper left.

111 Print from entire negative.

112 Reflection in door panel was selected as the subject for this picture.

113 The bas relief on the door serves as the subject for this print.

image is reflected. The picture is good as it is. For Fig. 112 the reflection was enlarged and made into an intriguing photograph. Fig. 113 features the figure as its subject. The two pictures (Fig. 112 and 113) are so different that no one would suspect their common origin from one negative.

While the illustrations for this chapter are necessarily few, they will give you some idea of handling composition when you start to make enlargements.

You must realize that there is no good and bad or right and wrong composition. What may be right to you may be all wrong to others (and vice versa). Therefore, as far as composition is concerned there is only one thing you can depend on: the way you *feel* about the enlargement when you make it. Ask yourself: Does it feel right? If it does, the print is O.K., the composition is as good as you are able to make it.

Print Contrast

What are the different grades of paper used for?

How do you utilize them in your work?

How can you control print contrast?

How contrasty should a given picture be?

To know the answers to these and similar questions is important because print contrast control is an essential part of enlarging, it alone often makes the difference between success and failure.

What Is Print Contrast?

Contrast in photographs *refers to the difference in tone between the different parts of the picture.* Fig. 114 is a simplified example. The pairs of tone pictures represent the tones of actual photographs. The top section consists of two tones: black and white. This pair shows the greatest possible difference, the highest contrast any photograph can have. The following pair shows a dark gray and a light

114

Simplified examples of print contrast. Top pair has extreme contrast, second pair shows marked contrast, third pair has little contrast, last pair shows no contrast at all.

115 Print with proper contrast, its tone values closely resemble those of the original subject.

116 This print is too flat, it lacks contrast.

gray segment, there is considerable difference in tone between the two, therefore this section shows high contrast. The difference in tone is slight between the two segments of the third pair, showing little contrast. The last two segments are identical, there is no difference between them, accordingly the last section has no contrast whatever.

For the sake of simplicity Fig. 114 shows the difference in the contrast of only a few tones. In an actual photograph, however, there are many different tones, which make it more difficult to recognize the degree of contrast present in the picture. The question arises: *How can you judge print contrast?*

What Is the Proper Contrast for Any Given Picture?

These questions are easier asked than answered, because there is no one rule applicable to every picture. We can give you three guides, though, which will help you to decide proper print contrast for practically any picture.

Guides for Deciding Proper Print Contrast.

1. Try to duplicate in your print the contrast present in the original subject. If the tone values in the picture correspond with those of the original subject, your print is most likely to have proper contrast.

66

117 Print with too much contrast, both highlight and shadow portions lack details.

118 Details have appeared in both areas when a softer print was made, this print has proper contrast.

The tones of Fig. 115, for example, closely resemble the actual tones of the live subject, the print has proper contrast. In Fig. 116 the tones are distorted, the print is gray over-all, neither the shadow nor the highlight portions are life-like. In other words, the print is flat, muddy, it does not have sufficient contrast, sufficient difference in tone between the light and dark areas of the picture.

2. Preserve both highlight and shadow detail in your prints. You can often test proper print contrast by checking the presence of detail in both highlights and shadows. If the highlights are "washed out," lack detail, and the shadows are black, also without detail, your print is too contrasty. Making a softer print, one with less contrast, will usually make details appear in both highlights and shadows. When we say highlight and shadow detail we mean such detail as is present in the corresponding areas of the negative. No amount of contrast manipulation will make details appear in those areas of the print which correspond to areas which are devoid of detail in the negative.

Fig. 117 has too much contrast, the highlight portions are "washed out," lack detail, as do the shadow portions, most of which are black. When Fig. 118, a softer print was made, details have appeared in both areas, the print has proper contrast.

3. *Your prints should be pleasing to view.* This is important, you will have to learn to judge whether the print is pleasing or not from the point of view of contrast. With a little practice you will be able to recognize a print which is too contrasty, too harsh, where the excessive contrast practically hurts the eye. You will learn to recognize, also, a print which is too flat or muddy, where the lack of contrast makes the whole picture uninteresting. Look at Figs. 119 and 120, two prints made from the same negative. The only difference between them is in print contrast: Fig. 119 has proper contrast while Fig. 120 is too flat, lacks contrast. A glance at the two reveals Fig. 119 as the one pleasing to look at.

Be fully aware then, of the fact that you have to *learn* to recognize good print quality. Many an amateur who fully understands how to control print contrast, still makes flat or overly contrasty prints because he has not learned to "see" the defects in his own work.

These three guides applied with care will *help* you to decide just how contrasty your prints should be. We say "help" you because there are several other factors to consider. Most of these have to do with the way the photograph was taken and with the effect desired in the print.

To bring out a certain mood, for example, you may want a print with either more or less contrast than you would aim for without that special effect in mind.

To develop your sense of proper print contrast it is also helpful to look at prints made by experts (exhibitors, magazine photographers, prize winners, etc). You may or may not like their pictures, but from the angle of print quality most of them are excellent.

Print Contrast Control.

By now you should be fully aware of the importance of print contrast and have a pretty good idea of what it is. Next you have to learn to *control* the contrast of *your* prints.

You will be making prints from negatives which may have different degrees of contrast because of variations in subject matter, lighting, film or development. While you aim to make negatives with just the proper contrast, as described in the chapter on negative making, some of your negatives may turn out to have great contrast and a few may have too little contrast. However, *regardless of the contrast of the negative you must produce prints with just the right contrast.*

You can control print contrast best by selecting the correct grade of enlarging paper. Most enlarging papers come in different contrast grades, usu-

119 Print has proper contrast, it is pleasing to look at. **120** This print is too flat, lacks contrast.

ally marked 1, 2, 3 and 4. Each of these numbers denotes a different degree of contrast "built into" the paper. Thus:

#1 is a soft paper.

#2 is a normal paper.

#3 is a hard paper.

#4 is an extra hard paper.

But these are only words and it would take too many of them to fully explain paper contrast, therefore let us explain by means of pictures instead.

Using Enlarging Papers of Different Contrast Grade.

For simplicity's sake we start with a negative which consists of equal portions of different densities, an artificial negative called a "gray scale" (Fig. 121), and make a print from it on each contrast grade of paper from 1 to 4.

The print made on #1, soft, paper is a "soft" print (Fig. 122). The dark parts are not quite dark and the light parts not quite light. There isn't as much difference, contrast, between the steps as there is in the negative. This means that a negative printed on #1 paper will yield a "softer than the negative" picture, one which has less contrast than the negative from which it was made.

On #2, normal, paper the print reproduces the difference, contrast, between steps approximately as it appears in the negative (Fig. 123). Accordingly, a #2, normal, paper does not change the contrast of the negative.

Fig. 124 shows a print on #3, hard, paper. In this print there is a greater difference between steps than there is in the negative and you can see how #3 paper increases, in the print, the contrast present in the negative.

121   Gray scale negative.

In Fig. 125 the print was made on #4, extra hard, paper. Here the contrast between each step is much greater than in the negative. The #4 paper has greatly increased, in the print, the contrast present in the negative.

Let us repeat our gray scale experiment with an actual picture. Fig. 126 is a negative with normal contrast. We have made prints from it on #1, #2, #3 and #4 paper and see that the results are similar to our experiments with the gray scale.

On #1 paper (Fig. 127) the print shows very little difference between the light and dark parts, it has very little contrast. It is a bad print, flat and muddy.

The print on #2 paper has a greater difference, greater contrast between light and dark parts. It is a good print (Fig. 128). This is the paper that "fits" this negative.

On #3 paper the print shows a still greater, somewhat exaggerated difference between light and dark parts, it is a little too contrasty, too hard (Fig. 129).

The last print (Fig. 130) was made on #4 paper. Here the contrast is so great that the picture actually consists of very dark and very light parts only, the middle tones are missing and the details are lost in both highlight and shadow areas. The #4 paper has greatly exaggerated the contrast.

Study the illustrations to see what the different contrast grades of paper will do for you in your enlarging work. By now you should know the difference between #1, #2, #3 and #4 papers.

So far we have made prints on #1, #2, #3 and #4 papers, but only the one made on #2 turned out to be good. The rest were either too soft or too hard. This happened because we used a *normal* negative, one with "medium" contrast in making the prints. The paper grades, other than #2, are utilized to compensate for differences in negative contrast, to produce "normal" prints from negatives of other than normal contrast.

122 Print from gray scale negative on #1 paper has softer gradation than the negative.

123 Print on #2 paper has about the same gradation as the negative.

124 Print on #3 paper shows more difference in tone between steps, has more contrast than the negative.

125 On #4 paper the contrast between each step is much greater than on the negative.

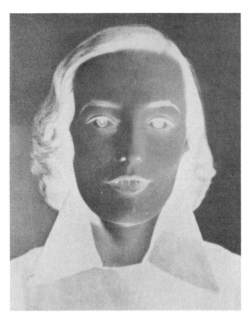

126
Negative with normal contrast.

Paper Grades Compensate for Differences In Negative Contrast.

If you have a *very contrasty negative* the print made from it on normal (#2) paper also would be very contrasty. But if you use a soft (#1) paper which *decreases the contrast* present in the negative, you will approximate a normal print.

If you have a *normal contrast negative* you may print it on normal (#2) paper and get a normal print.

If you have a *flat negative,* one which has little contrast, the print made from it on normal (#2) paper would also be flat. To get a normal print from such a negative you will have to use a paper which *increases, in the print, the contrast present in the negative,* a hard paper (#3).

Finally you may have a *very flat negative,* one which has very little contrast. With #4, extra hard paper, which *greatly increases the contrast* present in the negative, you still will be able to make an acceptable print.

Let us put this into practice. Fig. 131 is a normal negative, a print made from it on normal (#2) paper is satisfactory (Fig. 132).

Fig. 133 shows a negative that is too contrasty. The print made from it on normal (#2) paper is also too contrasty (Fig. 134). On #1 paper we obtain an acceptable print, thanks to the contrast decreasing property of the #1 paper (Fig. 135).

Fig. 136 shows a soft negative, one with little contrast. Printed on #2, normal paper, the picture is too soft, too flat (Fig. 137). It takes the contrast

127   Print made on #1 paper is flat and muddy.   **128**   Print made on #2 paper is just about right.

129   Print made on #3 paper is too contrasty.   **130**   Print made on #4 paper is much too contrasty.

131 Normal negative.

132 Satisfactory print was made on normal (#2) paper.

increasing, hard (#3) paper to make a suitable print from this negative (Fig. 138).

Fig. 139 shows a very flat negative. Printed on #2, normal paper, it yields a muddy, flat picture (Fig. 140). It takes the very high contrast of a #4, extra-hard paper to make a satisfactory print from this negative (Fig. 141).

From the above illustrations you see that you can produce good prints on #1, #2, #3 and #4 papers, if the contrast of the paper fits the contrast of the negative.

You now understand that papers of different contrast are provided to make it possible for you to produce good prints from negatives which have normal, too much or too little contrast.

Many papers, mostly the slow chlorobromides (the so-called warm tone papers), are not made in the full range of contrast grades. Some are offered in only one grade, #2, others in two grades. To use such papers successfully the contrast of the negatives should fit the contrast of the paper.

One paper, Kodabromide, is made also in a #5 grade. Those who use Kodabromide will utilize the #5 grade to get maximum contrast in the print.

The contrast of another paper, Du Pont's "Varigam," is controlled by the

133 Contrasty negative.　　**134** Print on #2 paper is too contrasty.　　**135** Print on #1 paper is about right.

136 Flat negative.　　**137** Print on #2 paper is too flat.　　**138** Print on #3 paper is about right.

139 Very flat negative.　　**140** Print on #2 paper is very flat.　　**141** Print on #4 paper is about right.

use of colored filters placed in front of the lens of the enlarger. "Varigam" enables you to buy and stock only one paper and still have a wide range of contrast to match your negatives. There are ten "Varigam" filters, numbered from 1 to 10. #1 yields the softest results, makes prints about a full grade softer than those made on regular #1 paper. Each higher numbered filter increases contrast in the print. #10 the most contrasty yields prints which are a little harder than prints made on regular #3 paper, but not quite as hard as those made on regular #4 paper. However, the ten "Varigam" filters allow you more control over print contrast than the regular four grades of enlarging papers, except when you have a *very* flat negative, for which you will still have to use a regular #4 paper.

"Varigam" paper has a unique advantage, one which is not offered by any other paper: it enables you to obtain more than one degree of contrast in the making of a single print. In other words, you can obtain a different contrast in different parts of the same print simply by changing filters while printing those different parts separately. This technique is described in Chapter X, which explains dodging and burning in.

The apparent contrast of a print is influenced by the paper surface used. All other factors being equal, a print made on glossy paper will appear to be more contrasty than one made on a semi-matte, while the latter will still show more contrast than a print made on matte paper. All prints appear to be more contrasty while wet than when dry, except ferrotyped glossies.

The amount of print exposure, the developer used and the degree of development have some effect on print contrast. These aspects of print contrast control are explained in Chapter IX.

Desirable Depth of Tone (Print Darkness)

Just how dark should any one of your prints be? What is the proper depth of tone for each print you make? To find the answer you have to consider several factors, such as:

1. The *actual tone values* of the original subject.
2. The *effect* desired.
3. The *mood* of the picture.
4. The *type of lighting* or other special technique used to take the picture.
5. *Special qualities of the subject* which should be emphasized.
6. The *purpose* of the print.
7. The *key* of the picture.
8. *Experiments.*

For the sake of clarity we describe these factors separately, although in actual work they usually overlap, several of them need to be considered for each print you make.

1. The Actual Tone Values of the Original Subject.

For many types of pictures print darkness will be correct if the tones of the print seem to match the actual tone values of the subject. According to this Fig. 142 is too light: flesh tones look darker than this to the eye, so this print does not show what the eye would see. Fig. 143 is about correct because in this print the flesh tones look natural. Fig. 144, on the other hand, is too dark: such deep flesh tones would only be natural for a person with an extremely dark complexion. Indeed, if we look at the three prints side by side, Fig. 143 is clearly the best, because it is the most natural picture.

2. The Effect Desired.

A good photograph has an effect on the viewer. The skilled photographer knows in advance what effect his picture should have and works to achieve that effect.

For example, Fig. 145 is a satisfactory portrait. We felt, however, that the picture would be more interesting if we could give it something of the qualities

142 Print is too light.　　**143** Correct depth of tone suggests values of original subject.　　**144** Print is too dark.

popularly associated with paintings by the old masters. This picture does not have that effect because the print is too light. The "old-master" quality of Fig. 146 was achieved simply by making a darker print. Here, we have departed from a natural rendition in order to create an effect.

3. The Mood of the Picture.

Closely related to the effect of the picture is the mood it will create. The two are closely related, but not the same. Before you can decide on how dark a print should be you must consider the mood of the picture, in addition to the effect it is to create.

Above we have achieved a desired effect simply by making the print darker. When we tried the same thing in Fig. 147 we did not get the same effect. Why?

The reason is fairly obvious: the mood of Fig. 147 makes it unsuitable for such treatment. The model is in a gay mood, smiling. A light print is suitable for such gaiety, not a dark one. The proper mood was established when the print was made lighter (Fig. 148).

4. The Type of Lighting or Other Special Technique Used to Take the Picture.

The depth of tone (darkness) of the print should be in keeping with the photographic technique used. Some techniques call for a fairly dark print, others for a lighter one. In other words, the depth of tone in the print should emphasize the qualities that are in keeping with the technique used.

For example, sidelighting was used to make Fig. 149. The main light was used on the left side with a weak fill-in light placed near the camera. The tone of the print is just right, the highlight area is fairly light, but not washed out, it shows texture and modeling, while other areas are dark, yet rich in

78

145 Light print does not fit mood of the subject.

146 A darker print reflects the somber mood of the model.

147 Dark print is unsuitable for gay model.

148 Light print retains cheerful mood of model.

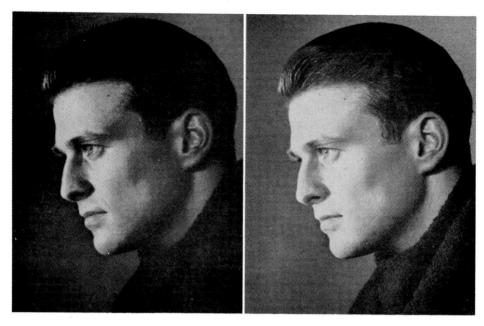

149 Side lighting was used to take this picture. **150** On this lighter print the lighting employed loses much of its effect.

detail. Fig. 150 is too light, it does not emphasize the typical quality of the lighting used to make the picture.

5. Special Qualities of the Subject.

It is often necessary to print to a certain depth, in order to bring out such qualities of the subject as texture, form, etc.

Fig. 151 shows the picture of a pelican just as it appeared to the eye in bright sunshine. While the picture approaches the actual values of the original subject, it is not good, looks washed out. Fig. 152, a darker print, shows richer texture and better form.

If the subject is not satisfactorily reproduced in the picture, changing the depth of tone may bring about an improvement. For example, to emphasize texture, or form, make the print slightly more contrasty and slightly darker than normal.

6. The Purpose of the Print.

If you know how the print is to be used you can make the print to fit the purpose. For instance, if the print is to be displayed under bright illumination it has to be printed darker than normal, otherwise it will look washed out under the strong light. Exhibition prints, for example, are made rather dark because they are judged and shown under bright lights. Conversely, if its place will be poorly illuminated, the print will have to be made lighter.

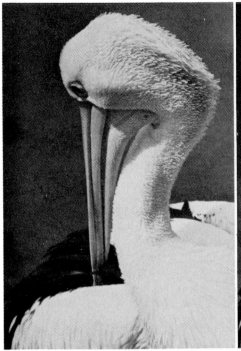

151 Form and texture are not properly shown in this light print.　　**152** Form and texture are emphasized in a darker print.

If the photograph is to be sold to a customer its darkness has to be just right to please the buyer, or there will be no sale. A picture made for reproduction will have to have just the right darkness for the engraver to make a good cut from it.

From these you can see that before you can decide on the correct darkness for any one print, you must know the purpose for which it will be used.

7. The Key of the Picture.

All photographs have a "key." Popularly speaking key refers to the proportion of light and dark areas in the picture. If a photograph consists almost wholly of very light tones we speak of it as a "high key" print. On the other hand, fairly dark tones predominate in a "low key" picture. If dark and light areas about equal each other, the print is in a "medium key."

Fig. 153 represents the tone distribution in a medium key print. Fig. 154 is a medium key picture, its light, middle and dark tones about equal each other in area.

Fig. 155 represents the tone distribution of a high key image. Fig. 156 is a high key print, the subject is only slightly darker than the very light back-

153 Average tone distribution in a medium key print. **154** Medium key picture.

ground. Fig. 157 shows what happened when Fig. 156 was printed too dark: the high key effect was completely lost.

Fig. 158 represents the tone distribution of a low key picture. Fig. 159 is a low key print, the center of interest stands out in lighter tones from the dark area occupying most of the picture. Fig. 160 has lost most of the low key effect because the print was made too light.

These illustrations show that it is necessary to print to just the right depth of tone in order to emphasize a high or low key effect.

Do not think, however, that a satisfactory high or low key picture can be made simply by printing any negative lighter or darker. The high or low key effect must be appropriate to the subject matter and the negative made so that the effect is in the negative. Proper printing only serves to bring it out, to emphasize it.

8. Experiments.

Do not hesitate to experiment with depth of tone. It often happens that a "too dark" or "too light" print will reveal a striking effect not apparent in the "normal" print. Through experimenting you will achieve improvement in some of your pictures and the practice will train your eye to perceive the most desirable depth of tone for each picture.

  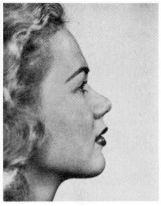

155 Average tone distribu- **156** High key print. **157** High key effect is lost
tion in a high key print. in a dark print.

158 Average tone distribu- **159** Low key print. **160** Lighter print does not
tion in a low key print. show low key effect
properly.

161 Fishing scene at sunset.

162 A darker print is more dramatic, suggesting a moonlit scene.

Fig. 161, for example, is a good print picturing fishing at sunset. Another print, made much darker, looks like a fishing scene by moonlight. The original scene was altered, a special effect achieved through a change in print darkness (Fig. 162).

Think carefully about each of the eight factors just described when you are deciding how dark a print should be for most effective presentation. Since each photograph is unique (as is each photographer) *you* must be the one to decide upon the depth of tone, for each of *your* prints. If you are in doubt at any time, do this: Make a print which you think is just right, then make a darker one, and a third which is lighter. When the prints are *dry* decide which one is best.

True depth of tone is revealed only when the print is dry. The wet print always appears to be lighter. If a matte or semi-matte paper is used the difference in darkness between the wet and dry print can be considerable.

All prints, of course, look darker under the safelight than they will under white light.

Making The Print

You are now ready to make a print. The procedure is surprisingly simple, but *you must follow the instructions carefully and exactly to get good results consistently.*

Make a Test Strip.

First make a small trial print from a section of the picture. This is called a *test strip.* Place a piece of the enlarging paper you think to be proper for the negative on the easel. Project the negative through the red safety filter of the enlarger so that you can see where you place your test strip. The most important part of the picture should be projected on it. For an 8x10" print use a strip about 2x4", for other sizes the strip should be in proportion.

Turn off the enlarger, push aside the red safety filter. Expose the test strip for a time you estimate to be right. The exposure must be timed *exactly* with your *audible* timer. As we mentioned before, the exposure should not be less than 10 seconds. If it turns out to be shorter, stop down the lens until you get an exposure of 10 seconds or more.

You have now exposed your first test strip for a certain *known* time. Before you develop it check the temperature of the developer (Fig. 163). It

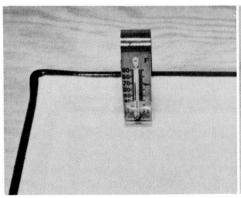

163 The temperature of the developer should be checked constantly. Thermometers which clip onto the edge of the tray are most practical for this purpose.

164 Double tray arrangement used for warming or cooling developer.

165-169 Series of test strips ranging from underexposure on the left to overexposure on the right with the strip in the center showing correct exposure.

can be anywhere between 65°F and 75°F, but *it must not change during work,* because that would cause inconsistent results. If the developer is colder than 65°F or warmer than 75°F you will have to adjust its temperature. This can be done rather simply by placing the developing tray into a larger tray which is then filled with water to ⅓ of its depth. To adjust the temperature of the developer hot water or ice cubes are added to the contents of the larger tray (not to the developer) (Fig. 164).

Agitate the test strip in the developer for exactly 2 minutes (2½ minutes if the developer is 65° or 66° F). Do this regardless of what it looks like. Whether the test strip remains entirely white or it turns completely black, *develop it fully.* Do not throw it away half developed, saying: "It's only a test strip." It is not "only" a test strip. It is *The Test Strip* which gives you *essential information* about the print you are going to make.

When the full prescribed time has elapsed rinse the test strip in the short stop for about 15 seconds, then put it in the hypo. Turn on the room light and inspect it. Do not inspect under the safelight, because the print will appear darker under such reduced illumination. At this stage you are interested only in exposure: is it correct, too much or too little?

If the darkness of the test strip appears to be just right, the exposure is correct. If the test strip remains white, much more exposure is needed (or you may be printing on the back of the paper instead of on the emulsion side). If the test strip is too light, give more exposure, if it is too dark, expose less. Always print the same part of the negative on a series of test strips (Fig. 165-169). Develop each test strip for the *full* time until you get one which is properly exposed, until the darkness of the test strip is exactly what you think it should be for that part of the picture.

170
Straight print made with the same exposure
as test strip in center of group at left. The
print is just right, no manipulation is needed.

Make a Straight Print.

The next step is to make a *full* test strip or, as you may call it, a *straight print*. Use a whole sheet of enlarging paper, expose it for the time indicated by your last test strip and develop it for the full time (Fig. 170). This *full* test print is *essential*. *Don't do any manipulation on this print,* even if it is obvious from the negative that dodging or burning in is necessary.

Study the full test strip carefully, make sure that the type of paper you use is proper for the picture, and that print contrast is what it should be. Then judge print darkness: is it right, too light or too dark? If the *overall* darkness of the print is incorrect adjust the exposure time accordingly. If the overall darkness is correct but *certain parts are too light or too dark* you will have to change the exposure time *locally,* you will have to do dodging, burning in or other manipulations (Fig. 171). The techniques involved are described in following chapters.

All manipulations must be timed exactly with the audible timer. Only if you timed all parts of the exposure exactly can you make proper and accurate exposure adjustments when required, or make an identical second print.

On your next print do all the manipulations you decided to do while studying the straight print. (These are described in detail in later chapters.) This should be a good print (Fig. 172). If you misjudged or incorrectly carried out the necessary manipulations and the print is not as good as it should be, study the print and decide upon the necessary adjustments, then make your

171 Straight print. Parts of the picture are too light, the bottom portion and the right side need to be darkened by burning in.

172 Final print shows improvement achieved by additional exposure given locally to light parts.

third print accordingly. It should be perfect. Your previous prints gave you all the necessary information about exposure and manipulations and if this third print is not perfect you have not followed the instructions carefully enough. The technique described is about as sure and simple as it is possible to make it.

Avoid Vibrations.

To make sharp prints the enlarger must remain completely motionless during exposure. Don't touch the enlarger, don't even move unnecessarily during exposure, the vibration caused by motion may result in a blurred print. A footswitch (available in photo supply stores) is best to turn the enlarger on and off, with a handswitch you have to be careful not to jar the enlarger.

Handling Prints in the Developer.

After exposure you immerse the enlarging paper in the developer, making sure that the solution covers the print quickly and evenly. The best way to do this is to hold the paper by the edge and push the opposite end into the developer, emulsion side up, then give it a quick shove, which will immerse the whole print in the developer (Fig. 173). Grab one corner with the tongs immediately and agitate the print vigorously during development (Fig. 174). If parts of the print stick out from the developer, push them under with the tongs.

When the full developing time has elapsed lift up the print by the corner with the tongs and hold it above the developing tray for 15 seconds to let it drain (Fig. 175), then put the print into the shortstop emulsion side down. *Never let the developing tongs touch the shortstop or hypo.*

173
Method of immersing print
in developer.

Handling Prints in the Shortstop.

Pick up the other pair of tongs quickly and agitate the print in the short-stop vigorously for about 20 seconds (Fig. 176). You may hear a sizzling noise and see bubbles emerge from the print. This is O.K.

After 25 seconds lift up the print with the tongs by the corner, let it drain for 10 seconds (Fig. 177), then immerse it in the hypo, emulsion side up. The same pair of tongs can be used in the shortstop and hypo.

The shortstop should have a vinegar-like odor. When the odor completely disappears the shortstop is exhausted, replace it with fresh solution.

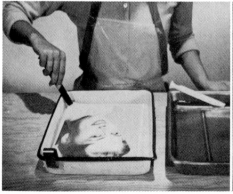

174 Print being developed.

175 Print is drained over developing tray.

176 Print is agitated in shortstop, emulsion side down.   **177** Print is drained over shortstop tray.

Prints in the Hypo.

Agitate the print in the hypo for the first 30 seconds (Fig. 178). After that it is sufficient to move the print once in every minute for about 8 minutes if the hypo is fresh, for 12 minutes in slightly used hypo, for 16 minutes if the hypo has been used several times. Do not overfix, prolonged fixing will bleach the prints. Some warm tone papers may start to bleach even during the pre-scribed fixing time. Fix such papers for less time and consult the instructions supplied with them about recommended fixing.

Lack of agitation in the hypo may cause spots. If there are several prints in the hypo, they have to be separated and agitated one by one, not together.

Both shortstop and hypo should be about the same temperature as the developer. If the temperature of the hypo is above 70 degrees, decrease fixing time about 25%.

The tongs are not practical for handling large prints (11x14″ and up). Use your hands to handle such prints in the solutions. Wear rubber gloves to prevent stain and possible skin irritation. Plenty of talcum powder in your over-sized rubber gloves will make them comfortable to wear. Handle prints carefully at all times. If your hands touch the shortstop or the hypo wash them thoroughly before placing in developer. Be sure that your hands are thoroughly dry and free of chemicals before proceeding with another print.

Washing Your Prints.

After fixing the prints are to be washed. *Complete and correct washing is important.* Use running cold water (about 62°F to 68°F), but do not let a forceful stream of water hit the prints directly. Wash single weight prints for at least one hour, double weight or large prints for at least two hours. The

178
Print is agitated in hypo,
emulsion side up.

time of washing starts when the last print from the hypo is put into the water. You cannot consider the prints as being washed while you keep adding others from the hypo.

Move and separate prints during washing, *the running water must reach both sides of all prints* for thorough washing.

You can wash your prints efficiently in a tray, or you may use a washer designed for the purpose. If you buy a washer, be sure that it is made of *stainless* steel, *not* galvanized, enameled or painted steel or iron.

After thorough washing the prints are ready to be dried.

Notes on Development.

To get good results you *must standardize* your developing procedure. *Use the same developer diluted the same way and develop your prints for the same length of time.* Deviate from your standard developing technique only if it is necessary to get a special result, but this will seldom happen.

Selection of Developer.

There are many good prepared developers available. They belong to one of two basic classes: 1. "Normal" or "standard" developers, like *Kodak Dektol, Ansco Vividol, Du Pont 53 D* and others (we use *Dektol* in most of our work). These developers produce prints with good contrast and cold black tone.

2. "Soft" or "warm tone" developers, like *Kodak Selectol, Ansco Ardol, Du Pont 51 D* and others. Prints developed in these have less contrast and the tone of the print is "warmer" than that of prints developed in a standard developer. The warmer tone means that the color of the print tends to be brownish

or greenish-brown black, especially if warm tone papers are used.

Dilution of Developer.

Most prepared developers are made up as a *Stock Solution,* which is to be diluted with water to make the *Working Solution* used to develop your prints. The instructions supplied with your developer contain all necessary information concerning its preparation. We dilute *Dektol* 1:2, which means that we take one part of *Dektol Stock Solution* and add to it two parts of water to make the *Working Solution.* This is our standard developer which we use most of the time.

Dilute your developer as recommended in the instructions supplied with it.

Less than recommended dilution (adding less water) will make your developer work faster and produce somewhat contrastier prints.

More than recommended dilution (adding more water) will make your developer work slower and produce softer prints.

A change in the dilution of the developer will also change the tone of the print: a colder tone results when a concentrated developed is used, while the print will have a slightly warmer tone if the developer is diluted.

Developing Time.

Develop your prints fully, keep them in the developer for the entire standard developing time. This is the very important basic rule of quality printing. Standard developing time for most developers is 2 minutes (2½ minutes if the developer is 65°F or 66°F). You can get *consistently good results* only if you develop *every* test strip and *every* print *for the full two minutes.*

Fix it clearly in your mind that depth of tone is *controlled entirely by exposure, not* by variations of development time.

Slight underdevelopment will result in a somewhat softer print, considerable underdevelopment will make the print look muddy and probably will cause streaks, due to uneven development.

Overdevelopment will slightly increase print contrast, if carried too far the print will be stained and sometimes fogged.

Variations in the length of development will also influence print tone: underdeveloped prints have a warmer tone than normally developed prints, overdeveloped prints have a colder tone.

Exhaustion of Developer.

If you make a great number of prints the developer may become exhausted, you will have to mix a new batch. There is no specific test to tell you when this happens, yet you can tell easily enough: the developing action slows down noticeably, the solution becomes brownish and foams readily.

Dodging and Burning In

Local control of the amount of exposure in enlarging is called dodging and burning in.

It would be ideal if you could put your negative into the enlarger, expose the paper, develop and have a perfect print, but it is seldom so. When the overall exposure is correct for the print, usually there are some areas which are darker or lighter than you want them. In order to bring these areas to the desired tone you will have to "dodge" or "hold back" the darker ones and "burn in" those that are too light.

Dodging or *decreasing the exposure time locally* has to be done *during* the overall exposure, as you want to give *less* than the overall exposure at those spots.

Burning in or *increasing the exposure time locally* has to be done *after* the overall exposure is completed, as you want to give *more* than the overall exposure to those parts.

Tools to be Used.

You need only a few simple home made tools. They are shown in Figs. 179 and 180. There are two 10″ long wire handles which accomodate a series of cardboard pieces of different sizes and shapes. These are the dodgers. The ones shown in Fig. 179 are usually sufficient, but you can cut out others of any size and shape that you may need for a particular dodging job. Several pieces of 8x10″ cardboard are also needed for burning in. Two of them are solid, the rest have holes of different sizes and shapes.

That is about all the equipment you need for 8x10″ enlargements. For larger or smaller sizes, larger or smaller dodger sets should be used for best results. The cardboard used to make them has to be dark in color and dull in finish to prevent reflections which could fog your prints.

Sometimes you will use your hands for dodging or burning in.

The Principle of the Spreading Shadow.

You have to learn to use these tools, including your hands. Start without a negative. The first thing to be learned is *the principle of the spreading shad-*

179 Set of dodgers.   **180** Cardboards with holes, used for burning in.

ow. An understanding of this principle will not only help you to do a good job of dodging and burning in, but it also will help you out if something goes wrong, you will be able to recognize the mistake you made and decide how to correct it.

When you hold a dodging disc between the lens and the enlarging paper it will cast a shadow. The *size and sharpness* of the shadow depends upon the *height* at which you hold the dodger. The higher you lift it (nearer to the lens) the larger its shadow will be, and also the more blurred the shadow will become. The lower you hold it (nearer to the paper) the smaller its shadow will be and the sharper it will become. This is illustrated in Figs. 181 to 184.

The same principle is true for burning in. A cardboard with a small hole held high will produce a circle of light with a blurred, blended edge. If you hold a cardboard with a large hole low, the resulting circle of light will have sharp edges (Figs. 185 to 188).

The principle of the spreading shadow also holds true when you have a negative in the enlarger, although most of the time it is not visible when you look at the projected image. But you will have to consider it, nevertheless, when you dodge or burn in to be able to get sharp or blended edges at will.

The opening (f:stop) of the enlarger lens also influences the amount of blending. The spreading of the shadow decreases as the lens is stopped down.

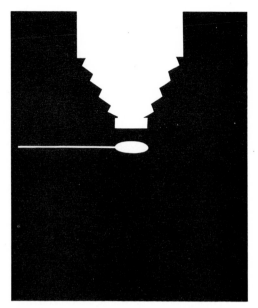

181 Small dodger held high . . .

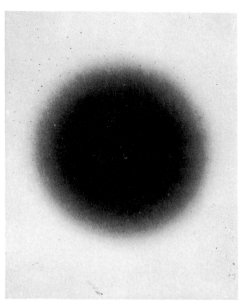

182 . . . casts a large shadow with blurred edges.

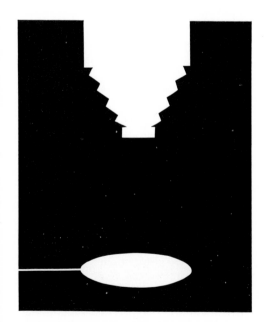

183 Large dodger held low . . .

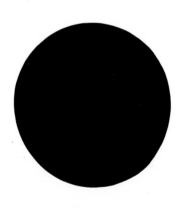

184 . . . casts a large shadow with sharp edges.

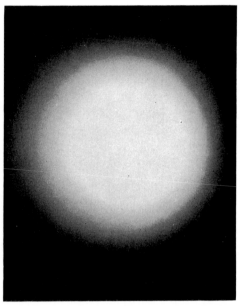

185 Cardboard with small hole held high . . .

186 . . . produces a large circle of light with blurred edges.

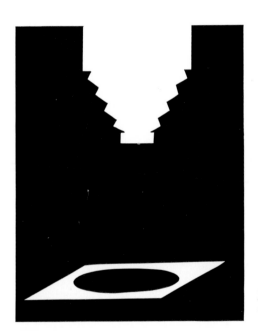

187 Cardboard with large hole held low . . .

188 . . . produces a large circle of light with sharp edges.

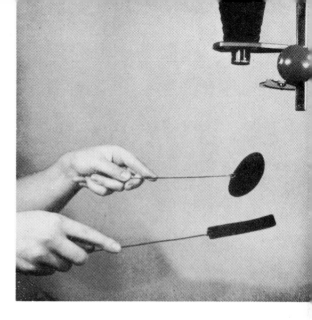

When to Dodge and Burn In.

Dodging should be done at the beginning of the exposure. If, for instance, you have an overall exposure of 15 seconds and you have to dodge for 5 seconds, don't do it from the 10th to the 15th second, at the end of the exposure time. While concentrating on the dodging you may forget to turn off the enlarger at the end of the exposure and thus ruin your print.

It may happen that the holding back times for various areas add up to more than the overall exposure time. In a case like that you use both hands at the same time to hold back different areas (Fig. 189), as the dodging time, obviously, cannot exceed the overall exposure time.

The necessary burning in can be handled at your convenience, part after part if more than one spot is to be burned in. While the overall exposure is the limit for holding back, there is no time limit on burning in.

The dodging or burning in time can be guessed or you can make test strips for each area to be dodged. The *difference* between the overall exposure and the proper exposure for the parts to be changed gives you the dodging or burning in time for each area. This difference is always to be deducted from the overall exposure for dodging (lightening) and added to it for burning in (darkening).

Using the Tools.

What tools do you use for any specific dodging or burning in job and how do you handle them?

The selection of tools depends on the position and size of the area to be changed in tone. You may use a cardboard, your hands or a dodger cut to the required shape and size.

To hold back (dodge) an area in the middle of the print use a dodger

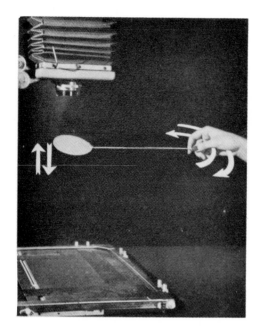

190

The motion to be performed with the dodger.

on a wire handle. The wire handle is necessary because the dark area is in the middle of the print and if you use your hand, the wrist and arm would cast a shadow, holding back parts you don't want to hold back. The shadow of the wire does not show on the print if it is handled according to the instructions given later. The size of the dodger should be about ⅔ the size of the area to be held back on the print, its shape should be approximately that of the part to be dodged.

When you dodge you have to be careful about two things: first, your dodging should not show, should be blended sufficiently, and second, the shadow of the wire should not leave a light streak leading out of the dodged area. Both of these are taken care of in one operation by the proper handling of the dodger.

Handling the Dodger.

To get the correct blending (which is partly taken care of by the spreading shadow of the dodger) move the dodger *vertically*. The up and down motion of the dodger is rather short, about 1/10 of the distance between lens and enlarging paper, more or less, depending on the amount of blending desired. Less up and down motion will result in sharper edges around the dodged area, more motion will result in blurred edges. However, if you raise the dodger too high, or move it up and down too much, you will get a so-called halo (light area around the dodged part). If you lower the dodger too far the center of the dodged area will be lighter than its edges.

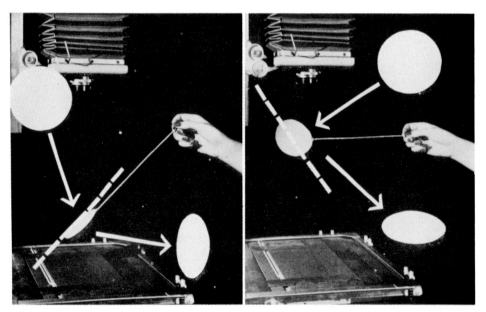

191-192 The shape of the shadow cast by the dodger can be altered by tilting and/or twisting the wire handle.

To avoid showing the shadow of the wire, move the end of the wire in your hand with a circular motion. The dodging disc remains directly above the area to be held back (being the center of the circle) while the wire is moved with the circular motion. Both movements (going up and down with the dodger and around with the wire) are done at the same time. The whole movement is easy after a little practice. Fig. 190 shows what the hand and the dodger have to do to perform the correct action.

The effective shape of any dodger can be changed by changing the angle at which it is held. For example, in Figs. 191 and 192 the shape of the dodger is circular. By tilting the wire to an angle (away from the horizontal) the shadow of the circle becomes an oval, getting more oval shaped as it is tilted more (Fig. 191). By turning the wire instead of tilting it, the change will take place in the other direction (Fig. 192). Because we can change their shape by tilting and turning, we can get along with only a few dodgers. With a few round, oval, square, oblong and triangle shaped cardboard pieces of different sizes you are able to cover an area of almost any shape, sometimes by combining two of them. When a very odd shape is to be held back you can cut out a piece of cardboard of similar shape and use it as a dodger.

How to Burn In.

Burning in (giving additional exposure locally) is done through a hole in the cardboard held between the lens and the enlarging paper, thus blocking

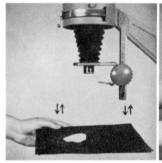 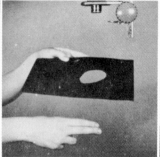 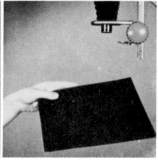

193 The motion to be performed with the cardboard during burning in. **194** The shape of the hole can be altered by holding the hand underneath. **195** A solid piece of cardboard can often be used for dodging or burning in.

the light everywhere, except on the area to be burned in, which is exposed through the hole. *The size and shape of the hole is important.* The hole has to be big enough to cover the *entire* area to be burned in without having to lift the cardboard too high. The height at which the cardboard should be held depends on the amount of blending wanted. The higher you lift it, the more blending you get. But lifting too high will cause uneven burning in, with a darker spot in the middle of the burned in area. Experience will teach you to decide the right height for every job. To begin with, it is safe to choose a hole big enough to cover the entire area to be darkened when the cardboard is held above the enlarging paper at about ⅓ of the distance between the paper and the lens. The cardboard with the hole has to be moved up and down *slightly* while burning in (Fig. 193).

The shape of the hole should be similar to the shape of the area to be darkened. If the shape is slightly different you can correct it simply by holding your hand between the cardboard and the enlarging paper, thus casting a shadow with the fingers on the part exposed by the improper shape of the cutout (Fig. 194). Hold your hand *between* the cardboard and the enlarging paper, don't stick your fingers into the hole in trying to change its shape to suit the subject.

If the area to be dodged or burned in has sharp edges you will have to keep the dodger or cardboard with the hole near the enlarging paper to avoid the blending of the edges. The size of the dodger or hole will have to be increased so as to cover the same area when held lower.

It is easier to carry out these local controls at the edge of the print than in the middle of it. Along the edges you can use your hands or a piece of cardboard (Fig. 195) freely without fear of causing light streaks. The hands are the most convenient and the most versatile in shape. By tilting them and changing the position of the fingers (Figs. 196-201) there are few shapes that

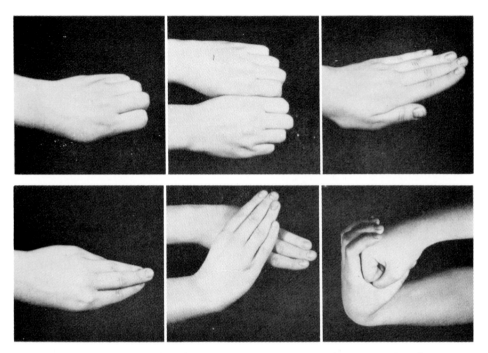

196-201 The hands are versatile dodging tools to be used on areas adjoining the edge of the picture.

cannot be covered. Do not try to use the hands if the size of the area to be altered is too large. If the area is too large, you would have to lift your hands quite high to produce a shadow big enough to cover it. This will produce a shadow with a very soft edge, causing excessive blending. Unless this is desirable, use a cardboard of the proper shape and size instead of your hands.

All these instructions may *seem* to be complicated, but they are not. You will find that they are easier to carry out than to read about.

Use Common Sense.

To do a good job of dodging and burning in, you need these instructions plus a little practice and a *lot of common sense.* Common sense will help you out when you are faced with a new problem, or when you are unsuccessful in your attempts to control exposure locally on certain parts of your print.

If in trouble start to *think:* do I have to darken or lighten this area, would more or less exposure bring it to the right density? How much blending is needed around the edge of the dodged or burned in area? What did I do wrong? If you ask yourself these and similar questions, you will find that the answers unfailingly will point to the proper technique to use.

Always time your exposures accurately with the audible timer. Unless you know exactly what exposures were given to each part, you cannot correct

202
The face is too dark in this straight print.

them if they turn out to be too much or too little.

Give yourself enough time, you need at least five seconds for each part to do an accurate dodging or burning in job. If the partial exposures are less than that, stop down the enlarger lens until you arrive at exposures of manageable length, even if this stopping down would make the overall exposure rather long.

And now an example: Fig. 202 is a straight print. The face of the girl is too dark. A considerably better picture resulted when the face was lightened by dodging (Fig. 203).

Errors and How to Avoid Them.

The use of a dodger which is too large or a small dodger held too high, results in a lighter ring (halo) around the dodged area (Fig. 204). The same error during burning in (too large hole or a small one held too high) would result in a darker ring around the burned in area.

A dodger which was too small and which was held too low produces insufficient dodging, only the center of the desired area has been lightened (Fig. 205). The same error during burning in (too small hole held too low) would result in insufficient burning in, only the center of the desired area would be darkened.

If the wire handle of the dodger is not moved sufficiently (or not at all) a light streak will project from the dodged area toward the edge of the print (Fig. 206).

Quite often the straight print of a negative which looks "impossible" can be turned into an acceptable picture by dodging, burning in, or both. Fig. 207

203 Picture is much improved when the face is lightened by dodging.

204 Too large a dodger, or a small dodger held too high, causes a halo, a light ring around dodged area.

205 Too small a dodger held too low causes insufficient dodging, only the center of the face is lightened.

206 When the wire handle is not moved a light streak connects the dodged area with the edge of the picture.

207 Straight print looks quite hopeless, face is black, branch above it is white, neither shows detail.

208 Dodging the face and burning in the branch have produced an acceptable print.

is such a picture. The sunlit part of the tree branch is washed out, the face of the girl in shadow under it is almost solid black. Great improvement was achieved by considerable dodging on the face and burning in on the tree (Fig. 208).

DuPont's "Varigam" paper has a unique property which can be utilized for local controls. Aside from requiring more or less exposure, parts of some prints could also be improved by changing the *contrast*. In graded papers the contrast remains the same for the whole of the print, only the exposure can be changed locally by dodging and burning in. With "Varigam," however, both *the exposure and the contrast* can be changed locally, simply by changing the "Varigam" filters which control contrast, for different parts of the exposure.*

No one can consider himself a competent printer unless he has fully mastered the twin techniques of dodging and burning in. Even though you fully understand what should be done, it takes practice to develop the dexterity which produces first class work. It also takes experience to sharpen your judgment as to just what local controls will produce the desired result. So deliberately plan on practice sessions in your darkroom—they are the one sure way to quick success.

*For full details see PRINTING WITH "VARIGAM," Camera Craft, $1.95.

Flashing

Flashing is another technique which can be used to improve your enlargements. It is done by exposing the enlarging paper to the raw light of the enlarger, with the negative removed, while the light is controlled to get the desired effect.

It is a *second* exposure which is applied *after* the print has been exposed to the negative image.

Flashing is used to darken parts of the print. Burning in is used for the same purpose, but it emphasizes details in the burned in part (unless you make it solid black), while flashing overlaps, hides the details in the flashed over area. Therefore flashing is used mainly where gradual darkening of the image toward the edges is desired, without emphasizing the details present in that part of the negative.

Factors to Be Controlled in Flashing.

There are three factors to be controlled in flashing: 1. The depth of tone of the flashed area. 2. The size and shape of the area flashed (you have to flash the desired area without exposing the adjoining parts of the picture). 3. The degree of blending. There can be an abrupt transition from flashed to unflashed areas, or a very gradual one.

Depth of tone is controlled by the duration of the exposure. The proper exposure time will have to be found by making test strips. With some experience a rather close guess can be made, but for beginners a test strip is necessary, just as it is for the straight print. Flashing usually runs from 1 to 30 seconds, depending on the speed of the enlarging paper used, the f:stop to which the enlarger lens is set, the light source of the enlarger, the distance between lens and paper when flashing and the density desired. The flashing time is entirely independent from the exposure given to the print, since the negative is removed for flashing. When the negative is taken out before flashing, the empty negative carrier must be replaced in the enlarger, otherwise a possible light leak may fog the print.

The control of the area to be flashed and the sharpness of the flashing are taken care of with one operation. This operation, which is the secret of success-

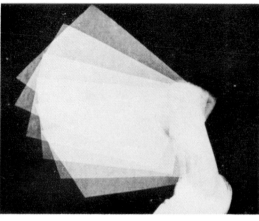

209 Proper way to hold cardboard for flashing.   **210** Motion to be performed with cardboard for flashing.

ful flashing, has to be understood and practiced until you can do it without difficulty.

Setting Up for Flashing.

Flashing is done with an oblong piece of opaque cardboard, about 8x10″ in size for 11x14″ or larger prints, 6x8″ in size for prints up to 8x10″. The underside of the cardboard should be dark in color and dull in finish to avoid fogging the print through reflection.

To learn flashing set up your enlarger as you would to make a print, but without a negative. Place a white paper on your easel to be able to see what you are doing, then start to work.

How to Hold the Cardboard.

Hold the cardboard as shown in Fig. 209, *not* in some other way, because this grip makes it easier to carry out the proper movement. While you hold the cardboard as illustrated, move your hand in a horizontal plane *from the wrist* back and forth without moving your arm. Only the hand moves, the arm does not (Fig. 210). Practice this movement for a little while until your hand gets used to it.

Basic Flashing.

In the *basic flashing* operation the tone of the print is deepened slightly *all around,* with well rounded corners and blended edges (Fig. 211). The ex-

106

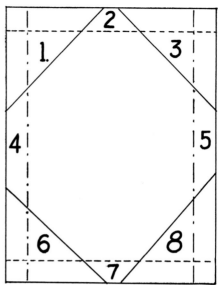

211 Result of basic flashing.

212 Diagram showing the order in which the sides and corners are to be flashed.

posure is confined to the outer parts of the print, the central portion remains unaffected. Of course, in actual work the flashing is superimposed, goes on top of the previous exposure from the negative. For learning purposes it is the best to omit the negative exposure and do the flashing only, so you can clearly see the result of your efforts.

To get the result shown in Fig. 211 it is necessary to flash eight times: once for each of the four sides and four corners. Let us go through the basic flashing operation step by step. Do it first on a sheet of ordinary white paper and when you think you can do it well, try it on a sheet of enlarging paper and develop it. The result should closely match Fig. 211.

First place numbers on a piece of white paper, as shown in Fig. 212. The top left corner is 1, the top edge is 2, the top right corner 3, the left side edge 4, the right side edge 5, the bottom left corner 6, the bottom edge 7, and the bottom right corner 8. It is important that you get used to flashing *in this order* all the time, otherwise you might forget to flash a side or a corner (or flash one more than once) and ruin your print. If you *always* flash in the above order, it will become a habit and you will not miss.

How to Flash.

To do the actual flashing, hold the cardboard in front of the lens of the enlarger (Fig. 213). Turn on the light of the enlarger. As the cardboard is between the lens and the easel, the light will not reach the paper. Now start

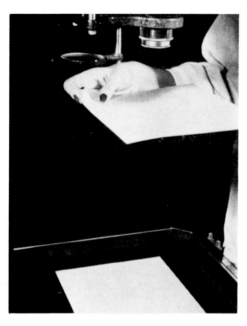

213
Cardboard held ready under lens of enlarger for flashing.

to move the cardboard as described above (from the wrist) so that with this movement you partially withdraw the cardboard from between the lens and the paper. Withdraw the cardboard enough so that the light is allowed to reach the area to be flashed, then move it back at once to cut out the light entirely. Then withdraw again, cover again. The cardboard is moved *all the time* by the swift motion of the wrist between the two extreme positions. This constant movement is very important as it helps you to get proper blending. Another factor which influences blending is the *height* at which the cardboard is held. The closer to the lens you hold the cardboard during flashing the more blending you get. In average work the cardboard is held about 3 or 4 inches under the lens, a little more for large prints. If some part of the enlarger interferes with the proper motion of the flashing cardboard, use a smaller piece of cardboard or tilt it to avoid the interfering part.

To get results similar to Fig. 211 follow the diagram in Fig. 214, which shows how far to withdraw the cardboard for all the eight positions. Withdraw the cardboard a little beyond the point at which you want the effect to terminate. Only experience can teach you just how far to go to get any desired effect.

Give the exposure decided by test to all eight positions. When you flash positions 4 and 5 (the two sides) change your grip on the cardboard. You can perform the proper movement easier if instead of holding it by the corner you hold it at the middle of the bottom edge, as shown in Fig. 215.

Try to establish a consistent rhythm, or speed, at which the card is moved

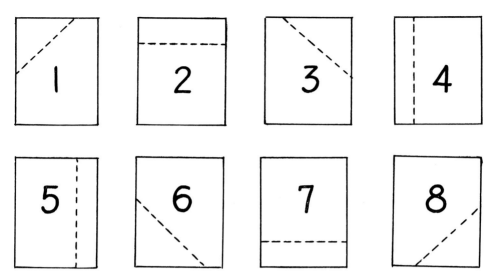

214 Diagram shows how far to withdraw the cardboard in proportion to the size of the print for each of the eight positions.

back and forth, and maintain that rhythm at all times. Then the amount of effective exposure will always be the same over a given period of time. If the card is moved more slowly at one time than another there is no way to judge the amount of effective exposure. Slower movement will produce *more* effective exposure in a given time.

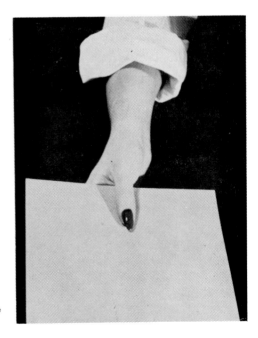

215
This is how the cardboard is held to flash the two sides of the print.

 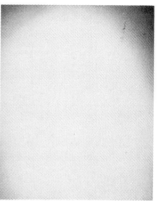

216 The background is too light in this portrait.　**217** Flashed print.　**218** Flashing used on Fig. 217.

When you have developed the skill to produce a "print" similar to Fig. 211, go ahead and flash actual prints. When doing so it is necessary to remember where the subject is located on the print, it can't be seen during flashing because the negative has been removed from the enlarger. Usually it does no harm if the flashing overlaps the subject slightly but you do not want to fog the important parts of the subject.

While basic flashing calls for an equal exposure time on all sides and corners, you can adjust the exposures to make some darker than others, if desired. If in doubt, start with the basic flashing and study the result. If some sides or corners are lighter or darker than you want them, adjust the flashing exposure accordingly.

You will find many instances where this technique will improve or even save a picture. Any part of the print can be darkened and disturbing details

219 Straight print from entire negative.　**220** Blank corners appear when head is tilted.　**221** Blank corners filled in by flashing.　**222** Flashing used on Fig. 224.

  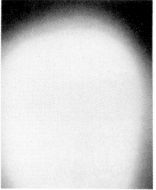

223 Top portion is too light.   **224** Print improved by flashing.   **225** Flashing used on Fig. 220.

can be hidden. Such treatment is often very helpful in "tightening up" a composition. The more you use flashing, the more uses you will find for it. Just don't be afraid to try it.

Examples.

We show just a few examples to clarify the application of this technique. Fig. 216 is a straight portrait. The background is too light, the picture has a sort of unfinished appearance. Proper flashing has darkened the background, concentrated attention on the face (Fig. 217). Fig. 218 shows the flashing alone, used on Fig. 216 to make Fig. 217.

Fig. 219 is a glamour shot. It did not turn out to be as good as we had hoped. We tried different compositions to improve the picture and finally settled on the arrangement shown in Fig. 220. The negative, however, does not have enough space above the head to permit this placement in a straight print. Flashing came to the rescue. Fig. 221 is the result. We feel that this low placement of the head, with the large area of black surrounding it, lends the picture a somewhat mysterious, exotic effect. Fig. 222 shows the flashing alone that was used on Fig. 220 to produce Fig. 221. The large black area of the print was flashed with a closed fist held above the area where the head was already printed. The right side, the bottom edge and the lower right corner were flashed with the cardboard.

Fig. 223 is also a "glamour portrait." The light area at the top spoils the picture. Burning in would have darkened it, but the design of the material would still remain to distract attention from the face. Flashing over the disturbing background made the picture more attractive (Fig. 224). Fig. 225 shows the flashing alone, used on Fig. 223 to make Fig. 224.

226

Flashlight used for flashing. It is moved along the edge of the print with swift, spiral motion. The distance between flashlight and paper should remain constant to get even flashing.

Flashing With a Flashlight.

While the best, most even flashing is done with the raw light of the enlarger, which is also the easiest to control, it is not the only light source that can be used. A properly equipped ordinary hand flashlight can also be employed. Properly equipped means that the glass of the flashlight is covered with a few layers of ordinary white tissue paper to decrease and diffuse the light, and that an opaque black paper shield is wrapped around its head to control the spreading of the light. The number of layers of tissue paper needed depends on the speed of the enlarging paper. For slow papers about three layers of tissue paper will be sufficient, for fast papers use about six or even more. We speak of thin tissue paper used for gift wrapping, not heavy tissues, like Kleenex and others similar to it. A trial exposure will quickly indicate how many layers are required.

Both the tissue paper and the black paper shield can be conveniently attached to the flashlight with scotch tape.

Fig. 226 shows the properly equipped flashlight in use and also indicates the motion to be performed with it. The flashlight is always held above the enlarging paper, pointing toward one edge and at a sharp angle. Never point the flashlight perpendicularly downward at the paper, you will fog your picture that way.

The flashlight is directed in turn toward each area which is to be darkened. It is moved about the easel so that the light is always pointed *from* the center of the print *toward* one edge. The flashlight must be kept moving in a circular or spiral-like fashion as it moves over the area being flashed—"painting" it with light. This double motion will result in even flashing. However, it is more difficult to achieve a smooth tone with the flashlight than with the raw light of the enlarger.

When the flashlight is used for flashing, the negative remains in the enlarger, and is projected on the paper through the red safety filter. Thus the image is visible and serves as guide.

Learn to do flashing properly. You will find it to be a valuable technique when you make fine prints.

Vignetting

The simple technique of vignetting can help you to make attractive prints. When you vignette you print through a hole in a cardboard. In the resulting print the image fades into a white background. Vignetting is usually applied to a head and shoulders portrait, but it can be used for other subjects.

You can buy a vignetter in which the size and shape of the hole is adjustable, or you can make one by cutting a hole in a cardboard. The vignetter should be about the same size as the print being made and should be dull black on the underside to prevent reflections.

Since the background is to be white, it makes vignetting easier if the subject is photographed against a white background.

To get a sufficiently white (dense) background in the negative place the subject in front of a white or light colored background and *throw more light on the background than the subject receives*. The shadow of the subject should not fall on the background within the picture area. Outdoors an overcast sky gives the best results: the lighting is soft and even and the sky background will be overexposed on the negative, just as you want it.

The background need not be absolutely white, a fairly light tone will vignette satisfactorily, but pictures with dark backgrounds seldom look attractive when vignetted.

Fig. 227 was taken with a vignetted print in mind. It is not bad as it is, but the vignetted variety looks more attractive, has a somewhat more "finished" appearance (Fig. 228).

Vignetting is also helpful when a negative includes details which you want to eliminate in the finished print. These may be other people, unsatisfactory surroundings, confusing background, etc. Cropping would be one way to eliminate the unwanted areas, but it is not always practical. You can print any part of any negative separately by vignetting it.

Fig. 229, for example, is not much of a picture as it is. A better picture was obtained when another print was made by vignetting the head (Fig. 230).

Fig. 231 shows the awkward result of vignetting a picture with a dark background.

227 Picture taken with a vignetted print in mind.   **228** Vignetted print made from Fig. 227.

Setting Up for Vignetting.

Place the negative in the negative carrier. If the negative is smaller than the opening of the negative carrier, cover the surrounding area with opaque paper, so that no stray light will be projected around it. This is important.

Next you adjust the vignetter. If you have one with an adjustable opening you shape the hole into an oval. If you use a plain cardboard for vignetting, cut an oval shaped hole in it. The shape of the hole should always *be an oval. Don't try to shape the vignetter to conform with the outline of the subject.* The *size* of the hole is also important. When you want to vignette head and shoulders, make the size of the hole such that only the face will be printed through it when you hold the vignetter about three inches above the easel. Hair, neck and shoulders should be blocked out by the vignetter. If the subject is not a head and shoulders portrait, the size of the hole should correspond to the area to be printed *with full density* (without *any* fading away).

Making the Print.

Now you are ready to make your vignetted print. Make the usual test strip, disregarding the fact that the picture will be vignetted. Once you know the exposure you can proceed to make the vignetted print. Put the enlarging paper in the easel, hold the vignetter above it and turn on the enlarger with

229 A rather unattractive picture.

230 A better picture resulted when the head in Fig. 229 was used to make a vignetted print.

231
Result of vignetting a picture with a dark background.

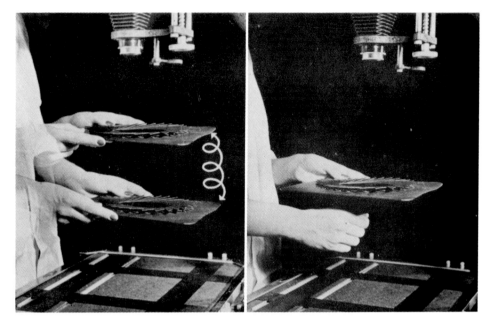

232 Motion to be performed with vignetter during exposure.   **233** Hand is held under vignetter for dodging.

the red safety filter in front of the lens. Adjust the position of the vignetter until you see the face projected through the hole. Push the red filter aside and make the exposure. As simple as that. However, the proper handling of the vignetter during exposure is important. It is not difficult, but the following instructions must be carried out exactly.

How to Vignette.

The vignetter is held with one or both hands. During exposure it must be moved up and down continuously with a slight rotating motion added to the up and down movement (Fig. 232). This motion is easy once you get used to it. In the beginning you should practice it without enlarging paper in the easel. When you can move the vignetter smoothly and correctly, then make the actual print.

It is also important that you know the highest and lowest point to which the vignetter should be moved during the exposure. Raise the vignetter toward the lens of the enlarger until you see projected on the easel an oval so large that it *almost* touches the margins of the enlarging paper, almost, but not quite. When you do this, the head, the shoulders, the upper part of the body and considerable background will be projected through the hole. When you come down with the vignetter, approach the enlarging paper with it until you cut out everything except the face of the subject. If you have followed these instructions carefully you should obtain a vignetted picture, similar to Figs. 228, 230 or 231.

If dodging or burning in is necessary on the vignetted image, do it the same way as you would without vignetting. Hold your hand (Fig. 233) or a dodger under the vignetter to do the dodging, while the other hand operates the vignetter as described above. For burning in simply disregard the vignetting and burn in the desired areas after the main exposure, the same as you would do on any other print.

Correcting Mistakes.

When you vignette a picture with a white background you can make mistakes to a limited degree and still have acceptable results. It is when you work with other than white backgrounds that your faulty vignetting technique shows up. One common mistake is the use of too large a hole. This allows too much background to show in the vignetted image, and the edges of the image drop off abruptly. Remedy: use a smaller hole.

Another common mistake is the use of too small a hole. This cuts out too much of the subject, only the center of the face is dark enough, all other parts are too light. They fade away to pure white too soon. Remedy: use a larger hole.

Vignetting is a simple process, it is easier to do than to read about. Go into your darkroom *now* and learn vignetting by doing it, by following the instructions exactly. You will be gratified by the fine results you get.

CHAPTER THIRTEEN

Multiple or Combination Printing

It is always the picture that counts. It makes no difference how you made it, as long as the picture is what it should be, what you want it to be. To get exactly the results you want, it may sometimes be necessary to combine two or more negatives into one print.

Multiple printing provides a method for making interesting pictures which could not be produced in any other way, and it affords excellent exercise in precision enlarging.

The techniques to be used are simple and you can learn them easily by following these step by step instructions.

Undetectable Double Printing.

In the first example we use two negatives to make an enlargement, which should look like a straight print, should not show that it was made from two negatives.

The negatives to be used have to be selected carefully, *the tone of the areas along the line of blending should match rather closely*. We combine the bottom part of Fig. 234 with the top part of Fig. 235. This will result in a print similar to Fig. 234, except that the clouds from Fig. 235 will fill the bare sky. The line of blending will run horizontally a little above the center of the picture. The sky tone of the two prints in this area is rather similar, therefore we should be able to do a good job of blending. A little difference in sky tone could be compensated for by exposure, by giving more or less exposure time to the two areas until they have the same tone, but great difference in tone would make smooth blending difficult.

It is also necessary that the two negatives should be printable on a paper of the same contrast grade, because the print will be made on a single sheet of enlarging paper. If, for best results, one negative requires #1 paper and the other #3, it is obvious that they cannot be made into a successful combination print. There is one exception: differences in the contrast of the negatives can be compensated for when Du Pont's "Varigam" paper is used. You can take a sheet of "Varigam" to make your combination print and use the appropriate "Varigam" filter to get the desired contrast from each negative. This is a

234-235 Pictures used to make combination print.

great advantage in multiple printing. "Varigam" will enable you to combine negatives which require different contrast grades of paper, a problem you could not solve in any other way.

Making the "Blueprint".

And now back to the example: we decided to make a combination print from Fig. 234 and 235. First we put the negative of Fig. 234 in the negative carrier, make the composition and focus on a sheet of white paper on the easel, then outline with a black pencil the parts which are to appear in the combination print. Then we repeat the same thing with the negative of Fig. 235. The resulting "blueprint" is shown in Fig. 236. Such a drawing is *essential* for *every* combination print, it enables you to adjust image size and composition properly each time you change negatives.

Test Strips and Exposures.

When the diagram is ready, the test strips are next. Make test strips separately for each part, including in each test strip some of the border area along which the two parts will be blended. Develop the test strips for *exactly* the same time, and be sure that the temperature of the developer does not change during the entire process of making the combination print. Inspect the test strips and adjust exposures until the areas to be blended match closely enough.

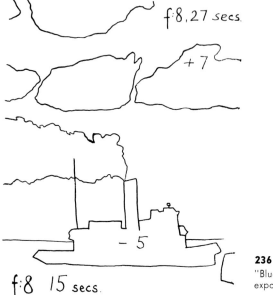

f:8, 27 secs.

+ 7

- 5

f:8 15 secs.

236
"Blueprint" showing placement of parts and exposures.

Mark the proper exposure data for each negative on the corresponding part of the diagram: the time and lens opening used, also any necessary dodging and burning in that may be required. In our example, for instance, an exposure of 15 seconds at f:8 was required for the bottom part and 27 seconds at f:8 for the top part. The boat had to be dodged for 5 seconds, marked as —5 on the diagram, the top of the cloud on the right side required 7 seconds burning in, marked as +7 on the diagram.

Making the Combination Print.

The "blueprint" thus completed, we can proceed to make the combination print. The bottom negative is placed in the enlarger, the image is projected onto the diagram on the easel, the outlines of the projected image have to match the corresponding lines on the diagram. This step assures proper image size and composition. We take a sheet of enlarging paper and mark one end of it on the back as "bottom." This provides a guide so the paper can be replaced on the easel in the proper position, without it you might print both parts of the combination on the same half of the paper. Use a soft (6B) lead pencil for marking and press lightly. The marked end of the paper is always placed in the same position on the easel, the lower image is to be printed on that end.

The first image can now be exposed: the enlarger is turned on and the exposure is made according to the test strip, but since the top part of the paper is not to be exposed, it is protected during the entire exposure with a piece of cardboard held about half way between lens and easel. The cardboard is cut

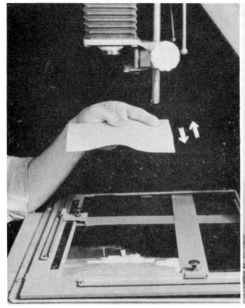 

237 Bottom part of combination print is being exposed. Cardboard is moved back and forth as indicated by arrows.

238 Bottom part would look like this, if it was developed separately.

out to match the shape of the area to be blended, a slightly wavy line in this case. The cardboard is to be moved in and out during exposure, toward and away from the area being exposed. Fig 237 shows how it is done. This operation results in a partially exposed paper. If we developed it at this stage it would look like Fig. 238. Of course, we don't develop it because the other negative is still to be printed on the unexposed top portion. Instead we return the half exposed sheet of enlarging paper to its box or envelope and change the negative in the enlarger. After composition and image size for the second negative are adjusted with the help of the diagram, the half exposed enlarging paper is again placed on the easel in the same position as before according to the marking on the back.

The second exposure is then made in the same way as the first one, except that now the top part is exposed and the bottom portion is shielded with a properly shaped moving cardboard (Fig. 239). This second portion, printed separately would look like Fig. 240. However, the two parts were printed on the same sheet of enlarging paper, making the combination print shown in Fig. 241. The picture looks natural, anyone who did not know how it was made would not suspect it to be a print from two separate negatives.

Check the Lighting.

Anyone who stops to think for a minute will quickly realize that subjects which are to be combined must be lit from the same general direction. A convincing result cannot be obtained, for example, if a foreground illuminated from the right is combined with a sky lit from the left. The lighting must be consistent throughout the picture.

As you can see, it is simple to make a combination print. All it requires is precision and calmness while you work. The crucial points are: the selection of compatible negatives, the developing of the test strips for an *equal* time, the *constant* temperature of the developer, and the *proper* use of the cardboards. If the cardboard cuts into the image being printed too much, there will be a light area where the two parts meet, if you fail to dodge close enough to the dividing line, there will be a dark area where the two images join. Remedy: dodge more carefully so that the area where the two images join receives the same exposure as the adjacent areas. We repeat, there is nothing difficult about these operations, but work slowly and think calmly if something goes wrong. Study the faulty print, if you make one, and it will show you what went wrong, so that you can do better on the next print.

Other Types of Combination Printing.

The combination print need not always appear to be made from one negative. Sometimes you will make combination prints which are obviously the result of multiple printing. The technique described above can also be used to make such prints. Fig. 242 is an example. It was made by combining Figs. 243 and 244 into one print.

Combination prints can also be made by "sandwiching" negatives. In this process you simply take two negatives, place one on top of the other and put them together in the negative carrier of the enlarger. The print itself is made as if only one negative was being used. Fig. 245 is a combination print made from sandwiched negatives. The sandwiched negatives printed separately are shown in Figs. 246 and 247. Negative sandwiching is a very simple way to do

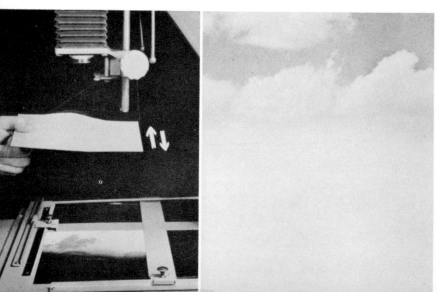

239
Top part of combination print is being exposed. Arrows indicate motion to be performed with cardboard.

240
Top part of combination print, developed separately, would look like this.

241   Finished combination print looks like straight photograph.

combination printing, but it is limited to negatives which give good results with this method.

You can also combine the two methods, negative sandwiching and double printing. For example, the three pictures shown in Figs. 248, 249 and 250 were thus combined to make Fig. 251. First the negatives of Figs. 248 and 249 were sandwiched, resulting in a print like Fig. 252. Before this print was developed, however, the bridge was printed on top of the sandwiched combination from the third negative. The bridge print alone would look like Fig. 253.

Silhouetted Foreground.

An easy variety of combination printing is used to introduce "silhouette foregrounds." For this type of multiple printing you need a negative which shows a dark subject appearing in front of a light background which is devoid of detail, like Fig. 254, where the trees are silhouetted against a blank sky.

242 Another combination print, obviously the result of double printing.

243-244 Pictures used to make Fig. 242.

245 Print from "sandwiched" negatives.

246-247 Pictures used to make Fig. 245.

248, 249 and 250 Photographs to be combined into one print.

251 Finished combination print.

252 Print made from sandwiched negatives of Figs. 248 and 249.

253 Bridge as printed for use in Fig. 251.

We combine this with the sky portion of Fig. 255. The result is shown in Fig. 256.

The printing in of a silhouetted foreground is perhaps the easiest kind of combination printing because practically no manipulation is needed. The two parts are simply printed on a single sheet of enlarging paper. The nature of the silhouetted picture makes this simple technique possible: the white background leaves unexposed space for details from the other negative, while the black portions cover the details from the other negative, thus eliminating the necessity of manipulation to provide empty space on which the parts from the

254 Trees are silhouetted against white sky.

255 Sky area is rather attractive on this photograph.

256 Combination print made from Figs. 254 and 255.

257 Artificial silhouette foreground picture, result of
table top setup.

258 Telephoto shot taken at the zoo.

259

Combination print with
silhouetted foreground
made from Figs. 257
and 258.

260, 261, 262 Pictures selected for combination print.

other negative can be printed.

In making such prints follow the same routine as for other combination prints: make the "blueprint" diagram, the test strips, mark the enlarging paper on the back, etc. The exposure for the silhouetted foreground negative should be the shortest which will produce good blacks in the silhouetted parts.

You may not have a suitable negative with silhouetted foreground on hand. In that case make one by photographing an unlighted table top setup in front of a white, strongly illuminated background. The resulting negative should be overdeveloped to increase contrast. Fig. 257, for example, was taken of small leaves and branches taped around an opening cut into a 16x20″ mounting board. This silhouette negative was then combined with Fig. 258, a telephoto shot taken at the zoo, to make Fig. 259, a "genuine" wildlife shot, apparently taken through an opening in the foliage used as cover.

Combination Print with Sharp Borders.

At times you may simply want to print several negatives on the same sheet of enlarging paper. It is easy. First decide on the arrangement of the separate pictures in the combination print. For instance, you might want to combine Figs. 260, 261 and 262 into a print like Fig. 263. The first step is to make a mask like the one shown in Fig. 264. It is a sheet of cardboard, as large as the combination print to be made, out of which pieces are cut so that you can uncover the area to be occupied by one picture while keeping all of the other areas covered. There are four pieces of cardboard altogether: the masks for the three pictures and the part covering the unprinted portion of the enlarging paper.

263   Finished combination print.

The masks are laid on the easel, then each of the three negatives are projected in their proper places one by one, in accordance with the previously planned composition. Test strips are made as for any other combination print. The step-by-step procedure goes like this. Negative #1 is placed in the enlarger, the enlarging paper on the easel is covered by the complete mask, and the piece marked 1 is removed. The first exposure is then made. Negatives #2 and #3 are printed similarly, each in its own place, while the masks cover all of the areas which are not being printed. This takes care of the prints of the three negatives. However, to make the print neater, it is desirable to print a black line around and between each image. To do this a narrow strip (about 1/16″) is cut off from each side of the masks numbered 1, 2 and 3. The trimmed masks are shown in Fig. 265. When these smaller pieces are replaced in the opening of mask #4 they will leave a narrow strip of enlarging paper uncovered around and between them. We turn on the enlarger, without a negative in the carrier, and expose these uncovered strips to the raw light of the enlarger. This will provide the black line between and around the pictures.

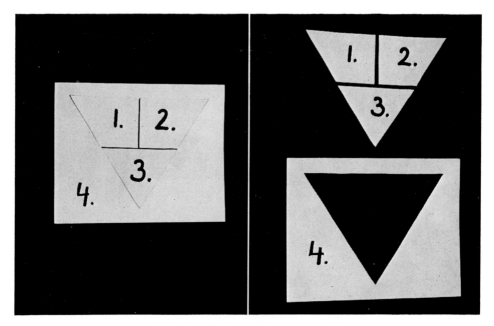

264 Masks used to make Fig. 263.

265 Masks used to make black lines between and around pictures on Fig. 263.

While the black line is being exposed, all cardboard masks must be in close contact with the enlarging paper, otherwise the light may get under the masks and fog the pictures.

To give a more finished appearance to the print we can make the area surrounding the pictures light gray, instead of white. To do this we remove mask #4, keeping the others in place, and turn on the light of the enlarger without a negative in it. For this exposure the lens of the enlarger should be stopped down considerably and the exposure time will have to be decided by test strip, to get exactly the tone desired.

Summary.

An endless variety of pictures can be created through combination printing. Your imagination and skill constitute the only limitations. The methods described here can be used to make any and every kind of combination print, no matter how unusual or complicated it is. The principles are the same whether two, three or a dozen negatives are used. Just repeat the same steps, once for each negative.

Here again, a certain amount of practice is necessary to acquire real skill. If your first attempt is not quite right, do it over until you can turn out a technically perfect job. And another thing—combination printing can be great fun. Try it and see.

Diffusion and Texture Screens

Generally you want your prints to be sharp, brilliant and rich in detail. Occasionally, however, you may come across a picture that can be improved by the use of diffusion or a texture screen, both of which hide detail and decrease contrast. An unretouched or badly retouched portrait, for instance, can be improved, made more presentable by the use of diffusion or a texture screen.

Types of Diffusers.

There are three kinds of diffusers in general use: the glass diffusion disc, the diffusing screen and wrinkled cellophane (Fig. 266). The glass diffusion disc is available in photo supply stores, diffusing screens are also available, but they can be home-made, too.

The use of a glass diffusion disc is very simple. Compose your picture and focus, *then* place the diffusion disc in front of the lens of the enlarger with the help of a slip-on holder, and make your test strip, straight print and final print as usual.

How to Make a Diffusing Screen.

You can make your own diffusing screen from any sheer material: a piece

266
Glass diffusion disk, diffusing screen and wrinkled cellophane, to be used in front of enlarger lens for diffusing prints.

267 Sharp camera lens emphasizes skin texture.   **268** Diffused print is sometimes more pleasing.

of discarded silk or nylon stocking, tulle, or similar fabric. Make a cardboard ring to fit around the lens of the enlarger, then stretch the material over the ring, securing it with a rubber band, and glue another paper ring around it. This is your diffuser. If tests show that it does not give sufficient diffusion, add another layer of material on top of the first one.

To make a print with your fabric diffuser compose and focus as usual, without the diffuser on the lens, then slip on the diffuser before you make the test strip. Different degrees of diffusion can be obtained by using the diffuser for only part of the exposure. For maximum diffusion leave the diffuser in front of the lens for the full exposure, for less diffusion give part of the exposure straight, without the diffuser. By varying the proportion of the straight and diffused parts of the exposure you can get any degree of diffusion desired. Be sure to make the test strip with the same amount of diffusion as the final print will have, otherwise it will not indicate print exposure accurately.

Diffusing with Cellophane.

You can also diffuse with a piece of cellophane taken from a package of cigarettes or a candy bar. Crumble it up into a tight ball, then straighten it out, but don't smooth it out. The wrinkled cellophane is an effective diffuser. To use it, hold the cellophane under the enlarger lens, keeping it in motion all

269 Sharp image.

270 Diffused with diffusing screen for the entire exposure.

the time. You can diffuse with the cellophane for the entire exposure or for only a part of the exposure.

Fig. 267 is a pleasing portrait, except that the sharpness of the camera lens over-emphasized skin texture. This may be desirable in some pictures, but for this particular print we prefer the smoothness of the diffused image (Fig. 268). A glass diffuser was used during the entire exposure.

Fig. 269 is a straight print. Fig 270 shows the effect of a fabric diffuser used during the entire exposure. The cellophane diffuser gives a similar effect. For less diffusion use the diffuser for only part of the exposure.

Diffusion should be used with restraint. Be sure that it fits the mood of the picture, and do not diffuse any more than is necessary to achieve the desired effect.

Texture Screens.

The texture screen, as its name implies, imparts an over-all texture to the enlargement. Various textures can be obtained to give the effect of an etching, a rough canvas, a paper negative, a bromoil print, etc. Texture screens can be purchased in photo supply stores as sheets of film, usually 11x14" in size, on which the texture has been photographed. They should be handled just as carefully as negatives.

To make a print you do everything as usual, except that you place the

271 Print made with texture screen laid on top of enlarging paper.

texture screen on top of the enlarging paper in the easel (dull emulsion side down, shiny side up) and cover it with a clean sheet of glass to hold it flat. Make the test strip with the screen in place. Once the correct exposure has been determined, you are ready to make the final print. With the texture screen in place you can use the same local controls (dodging, burning in, flashing, etc.) as you would use without it.

Fig. 271 was made with a texture screen called "dry point etching."

Home Made Texture Screens.

Smaller texture screens can be placed in contact with the negative in the negative carrier and the two then printed as a "sandwich" as described in Chapter 13. This type of texture screen is not available commercially, you have to make it yourself. With your home made texture screens you can make prints that are different from the standardized textures achieved with store bought texture screens.

To make your texture screen negatives simply photograph any textured material illuminated by cross lighting (with the light coming from one side

272 Negative of artist's canvas was sandwiched with negative of subject to get the texture in this print.

273 Single layer of Kleenex tissue sandwiched with the negative resulted in this texture.

at a sharp angle, just skimming the surface to be photographed), then place the resulting negative in contact with the negative of the picture you want to print. The two negatives should have about the same density. Place this negative sandwich in the enlarger and make your print as usual. The resulting enlargement will show the subject with the desired texture.

Keep the camera far enough away from the material so the texture will be quite small in the negative. This is necessary because the texture is enlarged to the same degree as the picture.

To make the texture screen for Fig. 272 a piece of artist's canvas was photographed and the resulting negative was sandwiched with that of the abandoned church.

It is also possible to use certain materials as texture screens. To get the intriguing texture in Fig. 273, for example, a single sheet of Kleenex tissue was placed in contact with the negative during enlarging (the box contains double layers, which must be separated to get a single layer for use as a texture screen). A piece of Kodak Dry Mounting Tissue in contact with the negative served as a texture screen for Fig. 274.

Another way to make an effective texture screen is to rub a soft (6B) lead pencil over the entire surface of a sheet of rough drawing paper (Fig. 276) and then photograph it. The resulting texture screen is placed in contact with

274 This texture was produced by sandwiching Kodak Dry Mounting Tissue with the negative.

275 Texture obtained by method shown in Fig. 276.

the negative to make prints resembling pencil drawings (Figs. 275 and 277). Texture screens are most suitable for subjects which do not contain large areas of dark tone. The texture shows most clearly in the middle tones.

You should learn to make and use texture screens as a part of your enlarging know-how. Employ texture screens with restraint. Use them only in cases where you feel that they really add something to the effectiveness of the particular picture.

276 Penciling over rough drawing paper and photographing the result produces an interesting texture.

277 Texture obtained by method shown in Fig. 276.

Border Printing

A print can often be "dressed up" effectively by printing a border directly onto the enlarging paper. Such a border can be solid black, solid gray, or it can carry a texture. If you are an amateur, border printing can help you to turn out prints which are attractively different, if you are a professional, you can offer your customers a variety of styles, and benefit because pictures with printed borders usually sell for more.

All that is needed is a sheet of cardboard with clean cut edges, larger in size than the print being made, and several sheets of black paper or cardboard to use for making masks.

Plain Black Border.

To make a plain black border, follow these steps:

Make print as usual. Leave enlarging paper on easel. Remove negative from enlarger. Take the large sheet of cardboard and lay it on top of the exposed enlarging paper, covering it completely, except for a narrow strip along the top edge (Fig. 278).

Turn on the enlarger and give enough exposure to make the exposed strip solid black. Make sure that the cardboard is in contact with the enlarging paper, otherwise the inside edge of the border will not be sharp. Turn off the light in the enlarger. Shift the cardboard so as to cover the part just exposed and uncover a narrow strip on the bottom. Expose it. Repeat the procedure for the two sides. Develop as usual. The resulting black border is shown in Fig. 279.

Black-White-Smooth Gray Border.

The next type we show is the black-white-smooth gray border. To make room for it the picture will have to have at least an inch of unexposed margin all around. For instance, on an 8x10″ paper the picture should occupy a 6x8″ area.

Make the print of the negative. Do not remove the enlarging paper from the easel after exposure. Make a black border around the print, as described above.

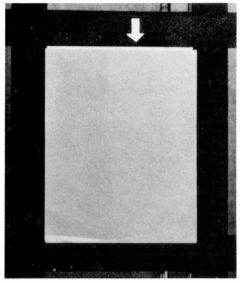

278 Exposed enlarging paper is covered with cardboard, only a narrow strip along the top edge is left uncovered.

279 Print with narrow black border.

Cut out a mask of opaque paper, about ⅛ of an inch larger all around than the size of the opening in the easel. In our case the opening was 6x8″, so the mask will be 6¼x8¼″. Place this mask on top of the enlarging paper in the easel, so that it *overlaps* the masking strips (margins) of the easel evenly all around. In the example the overlapping is ⅛ of an inch. This overlapping part of the mask will produce the white portion of the border between the black and the gray. Secure the mask in this position by placing some weight on it.

Now open up the masking strips of the easel to uncover the enlarging paper fully, except for the center area covered by the mask (Fig. 280). Remove the negative, push the red safety filter in front of the lens and stop down considerably, then raise the enlarger until its light will cover the entire area of the enlarging paper. Push aside the red safety filter and expose the uncovered edge of the enlarging paper to get a medium gray tone. The correct exposure time can be determined by a test strip.

Develop the print. What we have now is a black-white-smooth gray border all around (Fig. 281).

Black-White-Gray with a Texture Border.

The next class is the black-white-gray with a texture border. This is a very attractive variety.

We make the picture a little smaller to make room for a wider border.

280 Paper mask with weight on it covers center of the print, leaving margins uncovered for the exposure of the smooth gray border.

281 Print with black-white-smooth gray border.

282 Print with black-white-gray with a texture border.

283 Another example of printed borders. The texture in the gray part of the border is the result of exposure with a piece of Kodak Dry Mounting Tissue in the negative carrier.

The print will be 5½x6½" on 8x10" paper, the mask for printing the gray border 5¾x6¾". The procedure is the same as used to make the black-white-smooth gray border, with one exception: when the gray border is exposed some means is used to give it texture. This may be a texture screen laid on the enlarging paper, a texture negative placed in the negative carrier, or any other means you may want to use to give the exposed area texture. In our example (Fig. 282) we used a texture screen laid on top of the enlarging paper.

There is practically no end to the variations which can be obtained. Another example is shown in Fig. 283. The techniques you have already learned will start you off, your own inventiveness and imagination can help you from here on. Take your time when you make printed borders. First make your plans, then proceed slowly to give yourself a chance to do an accurate job.

Don't neglect the opportunities offered by border printing. Attractively printed borders often "give a lift" to an otherwise mediocre enlargement.

Photograms

What Is a Photogram?

Photograms are pictures made without the use of a camera, by exposing the enlarging paper directly to the light source. The picture is formed by placing an opaque, transparent or translucent object in the path of the light directed toward the paper or by manipulating the light in some other way.

You should learn to make photograms as part of your photographic education. You will not only get unusual pictures, but working with photograms will also increase your understanding of the behavior of light, photographic papers and developers.

Materials Needed.

In addition to your enlarger, chemicals and photographic paper, you need

284 Photogram made with opaque objects laid on enlarging paper.   **285** Setup shows how Fig. 284 was made.

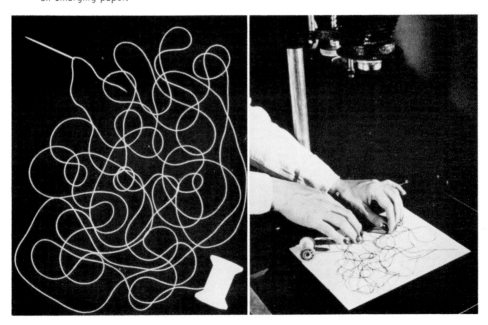

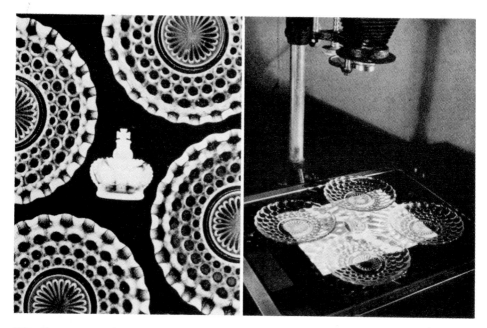

286 Photogram made with translucent objects laid on enlarging paper.

287 Setup showing how Fig. 286 was made.

a few assorted opaque, translucent and transparent objects for making photograms. Any photographic paper can be used: fast, slow, soft or contrasty. When you gain experience you will select the speed and contrast of the paper according to the results you want to get. In the beginning use any paper you have on hand.

Methods:

1. Opaque objects laid directly on the enlarging paper. This is the simplest way to make photograms. Stop down the enlarger to f:22 or smaller, then find out by making test strips what is the shortest exposure that will produce a solid black when the paper is fully developed. Place your opaque object on the enlarging paper on the easel and make the exposure. The developed print is the finished photogram.

Fig. 284 is a photogram made with the method just described. A spool, a needle and a maze of black thread was arranged on top of the enlarging paper to get this result. Fig. 285 shows the materials in the process of being arranged. You will notice that the thread did not lie flat on the enlarging paper. This was all right, because the stopped down enlarging lens still produced sharp shadows.

2. Transparent or translucent objects laid directly on the enlarging paper.

288 To make this photogram the asparagus fern was placed in the negative carrier of the enlarger, while the butterfly was laid directly on the enlarging paper.

289 For this photogram glass beads were placed on top of the condenser in the enlarger.

Such objects usually make good photograms because not only the outlines of the object, but its design and texture are also recorded. The result is often surprising, because the image may turn out to be quite different from what the object looked like when it was visually observed by transmitted light. The reason for this is that a translucent or transparent object also acts as an optical unit, bending the light rays to produce unusual effects.

Fig. 286 shows an example of this type of photogram. It was made by laying four glass saucers (bought in the 5 & 10 cent store) and an empty perfume bottle on top of the enlarging paper. The setup is shown in Fig. 287.

3. Mixing opaque and transparent or translucent objects. You can get interesting effects by mixing the two methods just described.

4. Object placed in the negative carrier. When the object is placed on the paper its image in the photogram will always appear in actual size. For a larger than life size image place the object in the negative carrier of the enlarger.

For example in Fig. 288 we wanted the asparagus fern to appear in larger than life size on the photogram. To achieve this we placed it between two glasses in the negative carrier and raised the enlarger until the image appeared on the easel in the desired size. The butterfly was placed directly on the paper.

5. Object placed on top of the condensers in the enlarger. Only flat objects

143

290
Cardboard masks, leaves and flashing were used to make this photogram.

can be placed in the negative carrier, others must be placed on top of the condensers in the enlarger if you want their enlarged image to appear in the photogram. You can get a sharp image of such an object by focusing with the lens (drive it up high) and by stopping down to a small aperture.

Fig. 289, for example, was made by projecting a string of cheap glass beads placed on top of the condensers in the enlarger.

This technique cannot be used with diffusion type enlargers.

6. *Special techniques: manipulating the light and the objects to get desired effects.* So far we have used the light as it came from the enlarger, resulting in an even tone all over, except where the object used to make the photogram modified the light. You can change that by manipulating the light source. Standard enlarging methods will do it: dodging, burning in, flashing, etc. You can also use additional light sources: flashlight, matches, etc.

The same is true for the objects used: you can move them around during exposure or manipulate them in any way to get the effect you want.

Figs. 290 and 291 are examples. Cardboard masks, natural leaves and flashing were used to make Fig. 290. Florist's wire and a tilted magnifying glass produced Fig. 291.

7. *Combining a photogram with an image from a negative.* This method offers further opportunity for experiment. The negative is placed in the negative carrier. The object which will produce the photogram part of the com-

144

291 Florist's wire laid on the enlarging paper produced the lines, a short exposure with the enlarger resulted in the gray background, while each one of the two black teardrop shapes was made by mounting a large magnifying glass in a cardboard and holding it tilted in the path of the light coming from the enlarger lens.

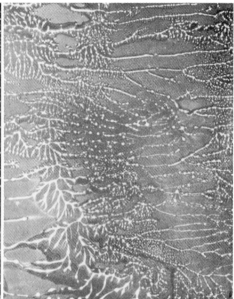

292 Photogram combined with a photograph. Negative and paint design on glass were sandwiched in negative carrier and printed together.

293 Paint design on glass used in making Fig. 292.

bination can be placed on the paper, in the negative carrier or on top of the condensers in the enlarger and the two printed simultaneously.

Fig. 292, for example, was made by sandwiching in the negative carrier, the portrait negative and a piece of glass with black oil paint smeared over it. The pattern in the paint was produced by pressing it against another sheet of glass, then separating the two. The pattern is shown separately in Fig. 293.

The above instructions and examples can start you off on a series of interesting experiments with photograms.

In photographic circles you may hear that a photogram is just a stunt; or that a photogram is not a photograph. Don't let these attitudes prevent you from trying this interesting field of photography, which holds surprises and unusual results for those who are willing to spend time, work, talent and imagination in exploring it.

How To Use New Coccine

Ansco's New Coccine is a red dye which, when applied to the negative, lightens areas which are too dark in the print or blocks out unwanted details completely. If you take full advantage of the possibilities it offers, New Coccine will be one of the most valuable darkroom aids you have. It is that good.

On many occasions certain parts of your prints are too dark. To lighten these areas you have to dodge them during exposure under the enlarger. This method has drawbacks: each print must be handled individually and if a number of duplicate prints are to be made, it is difficult to make them exactly alike. Also, if the tones of several small or oddly shaped areas need correcting, dodging becomes increasingly difficult, since all the dodging has to be crowded into the over-all exposure required by that print.

New Coccine may be used on all negatives from $2\frac{1}{4}$x$2\frac{1}{4}''$ up and, with practice, even on 35 mm. negatives. It eliminates the need for manipulation during printing. Once it is applied, any number of identical prints can be made. You can take all the time you need to apply New Coccine, and if you make a mistake during the process, it can be corrected. When the red dye is applied to the shadow areas, it decreases negative contrast, if it is applied to the highlight areas on flat negatives, it increases negative contrast.

Materials Needed.

Materials needed: a bottle of New Coccine, one empty 4 oz. bottle, four 2 oz. bottles, one $\frac{1}{2}$ oz. bottle, one eye dropper, one #3 finest sable hair spotting brush, one #oo finest sable hair spotting brush, about a dozen sheets of 4x5″ lintless photographic blotters, a box of Q-tips (or a supply of toothpicks with absorbent cotton wrapped around the tips), one pound bottle of 26% Ammonium Hydroxide (Ammonia Water, full strength), one small bottle of Aerosol or similar wetting agent, and one drawing pen (quill) with a fine point. In addition you need a working surface on which the negative can be viewed by transmitted light, such as a light box, retouching stand or just a piece of ground or opal glass with a 25 Watt bulb behind it. For small negatives a magnifying glass on a stand (like the one used by retouchers) is useful (Fig. 294).

Preparing the Materials.

New Coccine comes in powder form. Measure out 20 grains (not grams) and pour it into the four ounce bottle. To this add two ounces of warm water and shake the mixture a few times. The dye dissolves readily. Mark this solution *Stock Solution*. Measure out 15 grains of dye and put it into the ½ oz. bottle. Fill this bottle half way with water, shake, and mark it *Opaquing Solution*. Next, pour one ounce of water into each of the three 2 oz. bottles. From the 4 oz. bottle of stock solution take 12 drops (by the eye dropper) and add it to the one ounce of water in the first of the three 2 oz. bottles. Mark this *Working Solution A*. Add 24 drops to the second 2 oz. bottle and mark this *Working Solution B*. Add 48 drops of stock solution to the third 2 oz. bottle and label it *Working Solution C*. Add three drops of Aerosol to the stock solution and to each of the three working solutions. Do not add Aerosol to the opaquing solution in the ½ oz. bottle. Then, pour one ounce of full strength Ammonium Hydroxide into the empty two ounce bottle (don't inhale the fumes or let them get into your eyes). All ammonia bottles must be tightly closed, because otherwise it loses strength quickly. Even when you are working with it, open the bottle only long enough to dip your brush, then close it quickly.

Use any negative to start with. Make a straight, correctly exposed and fully developed print first. This is used as a comparison to check the progress of your work with New Coccine.

You can use any enlarging paper, including "Varigam." The color of the dye does not interfere with the action of the "Varigam" filters.

How to Apply New Coccine.

The dye is applied to the back (shiny side) of the negative. The dull emulsion side is laid directly on the glass in the illuminated viewer. Secure the negative with cellophane tape. Start with a thin area, one which appears too transparent on the negative and too dark on the print (Fig. 295).

All negatives, except 35 mm, have a gelatin coating on their backs. The idea is to make the gelatin absorb the dye applied to it. If done correctly, this produces an even layer of color which holds back the light during printing. The amount of light withheld depends upon the concentration of the dye solution you use (A, B or C) and upon how many times the dye is applied to the negative.

Most often poor results are caused by the dye remaining and drying on the surface instead of being absorbed by the negative. When this happens the wash of dye will be uneven and spotty.

New Coccine is applied with a brush, Q-tip or small wad of cotton, depending on the size of the area to be worked on. On average areas use the #3

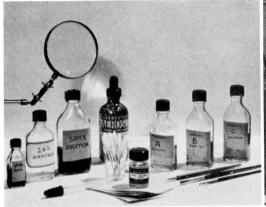

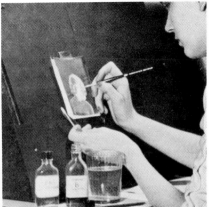

294 Materials used in applying New Coccine.   **295** New Coccine being applied.

brush. On small areas use the #oo brush. For very fine work, especially for drawing border lines in opaquing, use the pen, but use it lightly, avoid scratching.

For large areas on large size film use a Q-tip or a small wad of cotton. As a general rule, thin negatives are worked on with solution A, average negatives with solution B, dense negatives with solution C. When starting out, however, it is a good idea to use only working solution A, which gives you less opportunity to make a mess of the job. The wetting agent in the dye solution aids absorption, and you should help it along by *gently* massaging the surface with the *properly charged* brush or cotton. If there is any secret in applying New Coccine successfully, it is in the proper charging of the brush with the dye.

Dip the brush or cotton into the working solution, then remove the excess dye by wiping it on the blotter. This is done with a continuous pulling and twisting motion, which removes the excess dye from the brush. If you use cotton, dab it on the blotter. *The applicator of the dye,* whatever you use, *should never be wet, only damp with the dye.*

Handling the Applicator.

Once it touches the negative, the applicator must remain in uninterrupted contact with it, otherwise small droplets will form on the surface, causing spots. To avoid this, to get even results, move the brush or cotton back and forth without lifting it from the area, until the applicator becomes too dry to leave a droplet. This is why you should start with an almost dry applicator. If you need more dye on the area, wet your applicator again and work on it until a sufficient amount of dye is deposited. The finished negative must be left to dry

296 Print from negative before application of New Coccine.

for about 10 minutes, because the gelatin is swollen and sticky where the New Coccine was applied.

When dry, make a test print and examine the results. Probably there will be very little effect after one application of working solution A. Apply it again. Let it dry and make another test print. Apply again, if necessary. It may take several applications to build up sufficient density if the negative is heavy. Remember, this is practice, which will make you the master of the process. You are safer with the weak solution, it is less likely to produce uneven results. When you are experienced you will use working solutions B and C, which are more effective.

As a rule, you work on the back side of the negative, but there are times when you have to work on the emulsion side. For instance, if the back side does not absorb enough dye to get the desired effect, you may also apply the dye to the emulsion side. This will rarely happen, though. On 35 mm films

297 Print from same negative after the application of New Coccine. Compare with Fig. 296.

you must work on the emulsion side because there is no gelatin coating on the back.

To obtain a completely white area on the print use the opaquing solution on the negative.

How to Correct Mistakes.

At all times a slightly damp Q-tip should be at hand to remove any excess dye before it can do any damage. If you spread the dye into an area where it is not wanted, it can be immediately removed with the 26% ammonia solution. Dip a clean brush into the ammonia, remove the excess amount on the blotter and then work the brush over the area. Don't rub the brush too hard, because the ammonia softens the gelatin backing and may remove it completely. After a little while the negative gets dry and you can apply the ammonia again. Dip the brush in the ammonia for every application, because it loses

298 Both the highlight and the shadow areas of this picture were strengthened by applying New Coccine to the negative.

strength while you wait for the previous application to dry. *Never apply the ammonia on the emulsion side of the negative.*

If you make a mess of your negative with the dye, there is still no cause for alarm. Soak the negative in water for a few hours, or overnight, and the New Coccine will be removed. Sometimes a slight trace of red remains after soaking, but this usually has no effect on the printing quality of the negative.

299 Stray hairs at side of face are disturbing.   **300** Stray hairs were removed with opaquing solution, weaker solutions were applied to improve other parts.

If you want to remove the New Coccine completely, soak the negative in a solution of Potassium Metabisulphite until all color has disappeared. The solution is prepared from one part of the chemical dissolved in 20 parts of water (1 oz. Potassium Metabisulphite in 20 oz. water, for example). The film must be washed for ½ hour after treatment in this solution.

That's all there is to it. Follow the instructions carefully, work slowly and patiently. The surprising amount of improvement which can be achieved by the use of New Coccine makes it well worth your while to learn the process. This very excellent method for locally controlling the printing density of negatives deserves much more recognition than it currently receives.

Fig. 296 is a straight print from a negative in which the shadow areas are too thin. Fig. 297 was made from the same negative after the shadow areas were strengthened considerably with New Coccine.

On the negative of Fig. 298 the shadows were strengthened with New Coccine, and the red dye was also used to brighten up the highlights. In Fig. 299 the stray hairs along the face are disturbing. The opaquing solution was used on the negative to remove them and the weaker solutions were applied over the teeth, whites of the eyes and the highlights on the face to bring about further improvements. Fig. 300 shows the result.

301 Vignetted effect achieved with New Coccine.

Fig. 301 was "vignetted" with New Coccine. The background and the body of the girl were removed completely, stray hairs were cleaned up. Since the use of the opaquing solution results in sharply defined edges a weaker solution was used under the neck area to produce the necessary blending.

Print Intensification and Reduction

Intensification and reduction can greatly improve the quality of your prints. With these after treatments you can achieve effects which are not possible by other means. In addition to these special effects, you can, of course, save prints which are too light or too dark.

Print Intensification

Intensification does three things to a print: it increases overall print darkness, increases contrast and "warms up" the tone of the print.

The print to be intensified must be thoroughly washed, all traces of hypo must be removed. It is a good idea to wash it for an extra hour before intensification.

The intensifier is made up in two stock solutions:

Print Intensifier.

Stock Solution #1:

	Avoirdupois	Metric
Water (distilled)	16 oz.	500 cc.
Potassium Bichromate	1½ oz.	40 grams

Stock Solution #2:

	Avoirdupois	Metric
Water (distilled)	16 oz.	500 cc.
Hydrochloric Acid (full strength)	2½ oz.	75 cc.

Hydrochloric Acid is a powerful chemical. Handle it with care, don't let it touch your skin or clothing, don't let its fumes get into your eyes. Be sure *to pour the acid into the water gradually,* and not vice versa.

To prepare the *working solution* mix 3 parts of Stock Solution #1 with 6 parts of water, then add one part of Stock Solution #2. If only a little intensification is desired double the amount of water in the mixture (take 12 parts of water instead of 6). For maximum intensification use half the amount of water (use 3 parts instead of 6 parts).

Bleaching the Print.

The well washed print is immersed in the *working solution* (if already dry, soak it in water first for 20 minutes). Agitate the tray continuously until the entire image has bleached out. The bleached image is light yellow, its darkest parts are brownish. The bleaching must be even and complete, which may take anywhere from 2 to 10 minutes at 68°F.

The bleached print is yellow all over from the bichromate in the solution. Before further treatment can be given *the bichromate must be washed out of the print completely.* Wash the print for at least one hour in running water. If the water is colder than 68°F, wash it longer.

Redevelopment.

The well washed print is then redeveloped in your regular print developer (fresh) for at least 2 minutes, but not more than 5 minutes. After development the print is washed for 30 minutes in running cold water. No fixing is necessary.

Intensification usually softens the emulsion, therefore intensified prints must be handled with care, hang them up to dry, being careful not to touch the wet emulsion of the intensified print.

The entire process can be carried out by normal room illumination, but not by sunlight or strong artificial light.

If the print did not gain enough strength during the process, it can be intensified again the same way, but not before the print has been thoroughly dried first, otherwise the emulsion may become dangerously soft.

Any print can be intensified, but the exact effect of the intensifier on any one print cannot be accurately predicted. There will be variations in the results according to the paper and developer used, but these variations will not be very great.

The picture shown in Fig. 302 is too light, looks weak, washed out. To save it from the waste basket, the print was intensified with satisfactory results (Fig. 303).

Print Reduction.

When you inspect a print in the hypo, it may appear to be exactly as you want it. Disappointment often follows, however, when you look at the dry print. It may have lost the brilliance which made the wet print so attractive. The lost brilliance can be restored, most of the time, with a short rinse in a reducer, which is prepared in two stock solutions.

Print Reducer

Stock Solution #1:

	Avoirdupois	Metric
Water	10 oz.	250 cc.
Potassium Ferricyanide	2 oz.	50 grams

Stock Solution #2:

Water	20 oz.	500 cc.
Hypo crystals	5 oz.	125 grams

The print to be reduced must be thoroughly washed and, if already dry,

302 This print is too light.

303 Intensification produces pleasing depth of tone.

presoaked for 20 minutes before reduction. The *working solution* is prepared only when the print is ready for reduction, because it has a short life, it is effective for about 10 minutes only.

The composition of the *working solution* depends on the result desired. The stronger the solution is, the faster it will act, and for the same reason the more chance there is of spoiling the print by over-reduction. To begin with it is safe to mix one part of Stock Solution #1 with 100 parts of water and then add 10 parts of Stock Solution #2. The mixture is to be used immediately. Immerse the print quickly and agitate it for *5 seconds only*. Take it out without delay and place it in a tray of running water. When it is thoroughly rinsed, in about 1 minute, inspect the print, see if the highlights are sufficiently lightened. If not, return the print to the reducer for another 5 seconds, then rinse and inspect it as before. Don't try to inspect the print in the reducer, because the action may take place too fast and get out of control.

Always inspect the highlight parts, be sure that the highlight details in the print do not disappear. If the action is carried too far all highlight detail will be lost.

Prints on different brands of paper will react somewhat differently in the reducer. If reduction is too slow, leave your print in the running water and prepare a stronger *working solution* by taking only 50 or even 25 parts of water instead of the 100 parts used in the first *working solution*.

After sufficient reduction has taken place wash the print for 15 minutes in running water, then fix it for 5 minutes in a *plain* hypo solution prepared from 8 oz. of hypo crystals dissolved in 32 oz. (one quart) of water. *Do not use any other hypo.* After fixing wash the print for at least one hour in running water.

If the print shows a yellowish stain after reduction it means that you carried on reduction too long or that the print was not thoroughly washed before reduction.

Fig. 304 seemed to be satisfactory in the hypo, but when it dried the image appeared to be too dark. A short treatment in the reducer has lightened the entire picture somewhat, brightened up the highlights, resulted in a satisfactory print (Fig. 305).

Local Reduction.

While the brilliance of most prints can be increased by overall reduction, there are others which cannot be treated so because overall reduction would also lighten areas which you don't want to lighten. On such prints you can use *local* reduction instead. Local reduction can improve, or even rescue from the waste basket, many prints which contain areas that are too dark, dull highlights, blemishes, etc.

With this technique you can lighten any part of the print to any degree desired and, when the instructions are followed exactly, the process can be controlled with amazing accuracy.

Materials Needed.

You need the following items: a few pounds of hypo crystals, two fine sable hair spotting brushes (#3 and #00), several small pieces of blotting paper, one photographic viscose sponge, a supply of absorbent cotton, a small amount of saturated potassium ferricyanide solution, one eyedropper, one small glass dish (an ash tray will serve), one clean tray large enough to accomodate the prints you are going to work on, plenty of old newspapers, and sufficient working space on a table.

First prepare the saturated ferricyanide solution in a small (2 oz.) bottle. Pour one ounce of warm water into the bottle and keep adding potassium ferricyanide crystals to the water until no more will dissolve. There should always be a few undissolved crystals at the bottom of the bottle to assure a fully saturated solution. This is the *stock solution,* it can be stored for a long time in a well stoppered bottle.

Setting Up for Work.

Cover the table with several layers of newspaper and place the clean tray on them. Fill the tray to about 1 inch depth with plain hypo solution (see above). Place the glass dish, brushes, one piece of blotting paper, and a few small pieces of cotton on the table. Put one large wad of cotton into the

304 Print is too dark, highlights look "dirty".　**305** Short rinse in reducer lightened print, cleared up highlights.

hypo tray.

You can work on any fixed and well washed print, but not on one which has already been toned. The print must still be wet or, if already dry, resoaked for 20 minutes in cold water.

Prepare the reducing solution just before you start to work because it is short lived, has to be discarded and a new batch made about every 10 minutes. The reducer is made up by putting two drops of the saturated ferricyanide solution into the glass dish, and adding to it 4 eyedropperfuls of water and 1 eyedropperful of the hypo solution from the tray on the table. "Eyedropperful" means as much as the eyedropper will pick up at one squeeze and release of its rubber bulb, it is not actually full.

How to Work on the Print.

Place the wet print on the table and remove the water from its surface with a wet, but well squeezed out sponge. The brush or a swab of cotton is used to apply the reducer, depending on the size of the area to be worked on. On a very small area use the small brush, on a little larger area the larger brush, while on an extended area use the swab of cotton.

Dip the brush or cotton into the reducing solution in the glass dish, if cotton, squeeze it out well, if brush, wipe it on the piece of blotting paper to remove the excess amount of reducer. Now squeeze out the large piece of

306 Print is too dark.

307 Highlights were lightened, modeling emphasized by local reduction.

cotton in the hypo tray and hold it in the other hand.

Applying the Reducer.

The reducer must be applied with a constantly moving brush or cotton swab, unless the area to be lightened is very small. First apply the reducer for about 5 seconds, then wipe the reduced area with the hypo-soaked wad of cotton held in your other hand. Apply the reducer again, wipe again. Continue until the area becomes as light as you want it to be. When it is just right dip the wiping cotton into the hypo and carry some hypo solution over the area just reduced, let a small pool of hypo cover it. After about 20 seconds, squeeze out the cotton and mop up the excess hypo on the print.

Repeat the same procedure over all parts to be lightened. When there is no more reduction to be done, put the print into the hypo tray and agitate it there for 5 minutes, then wash it thoroughly. Reduced prints should not be dried on a heated or a belt drier because reducing may have softened the emulsion and heat or contact with the belt could damage it.

The print quality in Fig. 306 is rather poor, the highlights are veiled over, the picture looks muddy, flat. Much improvement resulted when the natural highlight areas were lightened by local reduction (Fig. 307).

Only the natural highlight areas should be lightened on any picture, because if other parts are reduced, the picture will look unnatural and the manipulation will be easily detected.

Figs. 308 and 309 show the motions to be performed to get satisfactory

308-309 Cycle of motions to be performed during local reduction: 1. Wipe area to be lightened with reducer charged applicator (cotton or brush). 2. Raise applicator. 3. Wipe same area with hypo soaked, well squeezed out wad of cotton. 4. Raise wad of cotton, then start all over again.

results. First the area to be lightened is "massaged" with the reducer charged cotton swab (or brush) for 5 seconds (Fig. 308), then the same area is wiped off immediately with the hypo-soaked-and-squeezed-out large wad of cotton held in the other hand (Fig. 309).

As you see the process is very simple. The "secret" is in the proper motion of the two hands: one applies the reducer with brush or cotton swab, the other wipes it with the hypo soaked, squeezed out cotton to stop reduction. After some practice these motions become almost automatic and make local reduction as simple as drawing on paper with pencil.

More Information on Local Reduction.

Every print will not respond in exactly the same way to local reduction. Some prints require a longer application of the reducer than others, or a more concentrated reducing solution should be used on them. We started with the standard concentration: 2 drops saturated ferricyanide solution, 4 eyedroppers water, 1 eyedropper hypo. If this works too slowly you can add another drop of the ferricyanide solution. If, on the other hand, the reducer works too fast, add one or two more eyedropperfuls of water. For best results the reducer should work slowly, but visibly.

Mix the reducer *before* placing the print on the table. Around the neck of the bottle there is always some fine ferricyanide powder as the result of evaporation of the solution. Although invisible, it may settle on the wet print and cause innumerable small white spots.

The print must be wet, but with no droplets of water on its surface. If you work on a print so long that it starts to dry, just flood the area being reduced with a little hypo from the tray. Saturate the cotton and then squeeze

310 Good picture, lifeless print.

311 Improved print has more life, more brilliance, resulitng from local reduction of highlights.

it out over the print. Spread the hypo with the cotton and after about one minute remove it, blot it up with the squeezed out cotton. In this process the print absorbs enough moisture to allow you to continue your work.

Controlling the Edge of the Reduced Area.

You may want to have either sharp or blended edges around the reduced area. To get a sharp edge just cover the desired area evenly with the reducer, wipe it, cover it again, etc., until sufficient reduction has taken place. To get a blended edge, start at the center of the area to be reduced and spread the reducer toward the edge with a spiral motion, wipe, start again at the center, etc. With this procedure the center of the area will have a little more time to reduce, to get lighter, resulting in an even blending around the edge.

If, when you finish working on an area, you find that a few spots remained unreduced or insufficiently reduced, don't despair, the print is not spoiled. You can continue to reduce these spots as if they were small separate areas to be reduced. If a few small areas become too light, or if you reduced small portions of adjoining areas, you can correct them when you spot the print later on.

Don't overdo local reduction. All work must be done with restraint, without spoiling the naturalness of the print. The method works so well that there is always a tendency to overdo it, especially in the beginning.

Once you master the process you will find countless uses for it. There is hardly a print which could not be improved by local reduction.

Fig. 310, for example, is a rather attractive picture, but the print is flat, lacks the sparkle present in the original scene. Carefully performed local reduction resulted in a much improved print, introduced the necessary brilliance. Highlights were lightened in the clouds, buildings, rocks and in the water (Fig. 311).

Toning

At one time or another most of us have seen a toned print which we thought was particularly good. Probably the appeal of the picture was due more to a happy combination of subject matter, mood and the color imparted by the toner, than to the toning itself. Nevertheless, we wanted to know exactly how that particular tone was obtained.

To answer such a question we must know every detail which had a bearing on the production of that print: the paper used, the developer, the exposure-development relation, the fixation, etc. Variations in any of these factors will change the results obtained with any given toner.

Since there are dozens upon dozens of toning formulas and preparations in more or less general use, the possible variations are far too numerous to mention, they would fill a book by themselves.

Therefore instead of telling you about all toners in general use we simply describe the few that we use most often in our work: the sepia, selenium and gold-chloride blue toners.

Sepia Toning.

We use Kodak Sepia Toner. It comes in a packet containing two foil envelopes. Contents of the larger envelope are dissolved in 32 oz. of water. This is the bleach. The completely washed wet print is immersed in the bleach and agitated there until the entire image becomes yellow or brownish yellow. This may take up to 15 minutes.

Wash the bleached print in running water for at least 5 minutes. While the print is washing prepare the toner. Dissolve the contents of the smaller foil envelope in 32 oz. of water. This solution has a rather unpleasant odor.

Immerse the bleached print in the toner. The action is fast, will be complete in about a minute or two. Remove the print from the toner when no more change is taking place.

The toned print should be washed for 30 minutes in running water and then dried.

The sepia toner should be used at a temperature of about 68°F. It works well with any paper, but the resulting color depends on the type of paper used. Toned bromide papers become a pleasing yellowish brown, fast chlorobromides turn to a somewhat purplish brown, while the color of sepia toned slow chlorobromides will be a rather unpleasant yellowish brown.

Selenium Toning.

Ready to use selenium toners are made both by Ansco (Ansco Flemish Toner) and Kodak (Kodak Rapid Selenium Toner). Both are stock solutions, to be diluted with water for use.

Selenium toners work best with slow chlorobromide papers, they have very little effect on fast chlorobromides and none at all on bromide papers.

The print must be wet when it is immersed in the toner (presoak it in water for 15 minutes if it is dry). The tone starts to change soon after immersion. Pull the print from the toner when it reaches the desired tone. Agitate the tray continuously to assure even toning. Tone at a temperature of about 68°F.

If maximum tone (reddish brown) is desired dilute the toner 1:3 (one part stock solution to three parts of water), for intermediate tones (purplish brown) dilute 1:8, to tone prints slightly (brownish black) dilute the toner 1:12.

The more dilute the toner is the slower it will act.

Gold Chloride Blue Toning.

The slow chlorobromide papers react to this toner very well, the fast chlorobromides tone slowly and only to a limited degree. It is not recommended for bromide papers.

First you have to make three stock solutions.

Gold Chloride Blue Toner

Stock Solution 1:

	Avoirdupois	Metric
Water	16 oz.	500.0 cc.
Thiocarbamide	¼ oz.	7.5 grams

Stock Solution 2:

Water	16 oz.	500.0 cc
Citric Acid	¼ oz.	7.75 cc.

Stock Solution 3:

Water	16 oz.	500.0 cc.
Gold Chloride	30 grains	2.0 grams

Each of the stock solutions should be kept in a separate brown bottle, well corked. They last for a long time (at least for 6 months).

All three chemicals dissolve readily. Handle the gold chloride with care: it leaves permanent stains.

To make up the toner for use take 12 oz. of water in a clean tray and add to it 1½ oz. of each of the three stock solutions in the order given above.

Immerse the well washed print in the toner and agitate it continuously. It will take from 5 minutes to an hour to complete the toning, depending on the paper used and on the tone wanted.

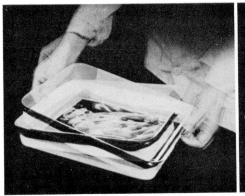

312-313 The tray should be rocked lengthwise and crosswise alternately during toning.

The toning is done at room temperature, but if a print does not tone well, you may raise the temperature of the toner to about 90°F to get faster action.

The print can be pulled from the blue toner when it reaches the desired tone. After toning wash the print for one hour in running water.

The gold chloride blue toner is widely used by salon exhibitors. Its popularity is the result of easy handling and pleasing, controllable results.

The three toners described will satisfy most of your toning needs. If you wish to delve more deeply into the subject of toning, a great variety of formulas are readily (and usually freely) available from the manufacturers of the papers you use and from manufacturers of photographic chemicals.

Hints About Toning.

There are a few things you should know about toning, which apply to all toners. The first is *cleanliness.* You must not allow anything used in the toning process, including the print, to be soiled with chemicals, fingerprints, etc. Hard rubber or glass trays are the best for toning, but enameled trays can also be used if they are not cracked or chipped. The trays must be kept scrupulously clean, and must be thoroughly washed both before and after use. The prints to be toned must be fixed in a non-hardening hypo (described in Chapter IV).

Prints must be *fully* washed before toning. Wash all prints to be toned for an *extra* hour, and be sure that they are separated frequently in the wash water.

As most toning processes soften the emulsion, dry toned prints by hanging, allow nothing to touch the wet emulsion.

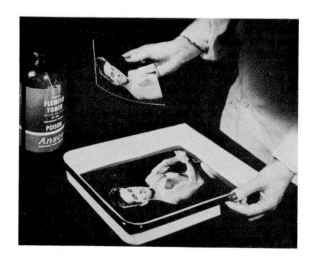

An untoned print can be compared with the print in the toner to see how far toning has progressed.

Follow carefully the instructions supplied with the enlarging paper and the toner you use.

Prints must be agitated in the toner continuously by rocking the tray alternately in two directions: along its length and width (Figs. 312 and 313).

It is a good idea to keep an untoned print handy. It can be compared with the print in the toner to see how far toning has progressed (Fig. 314).

Multiple Toning.

More than one toner can be used to tone different parts of the same print. While one part of the print is toned, a carefully applied coat of rubber cement protects the other parts from the toner. When the next part is to be toned the rubber cement is removed and the already toned part is protected by a coat of rubber cement. The protecting layer is always applied to a dry print, and can be removed by gentle rubbing from a dry print only. The print partially covered with rubber cement is soaked in water for about 20 minutes before toning, after toning it has to be fully washed and dried before the protective layer can be rubbed off. These steps are to be performed for each part separately toned. The back of the print should also be protected with rubber cement, which is removed only when all toning is completed.

Used with taste, toning can help you to make some prints more attractive, or to be able to sell them for a higher price.

Print Drying and Straightening

Once the prints are thoroughly washed the drying procedure begins.

Turn a tray upside down, wash the bottom of it clean. Take one print from the wash water, place it on the bottom of the upturned tray, emulsion side up, and wipe it with a wet but squeezed out viscose sponge (Fig. 315). This removes any dirt or scum which may have accumulated on the print during washing, and it also absorbs most of the water from the print. Be gentle, the wet emulsion is rather delicate. Rinse and squeeze out the sponge after every few prints. If you don't have a tray handy, spread wax paper on the table and place your prints on that for wiping.

When the prints are wiped off put them between sheets of lintless photographic blotters: one blotter, one print, one blotter, another print, and so on (Fig. 316). Keep on stacking them until all the prints are between blotters,

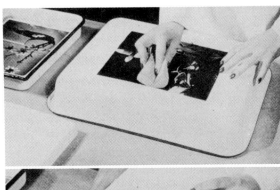

315
Fully washed print is placed on the bottom of an upturned tray and is wiped off with a squeezed out sponge.

316
Prints are placed between lintless photo blotters.

317
Prints being dried by hanging.

then apply pressure on the top blotter to make good contact between prints and blotters to absorb all surface moisture.

If you have a dryer, take the prints from between the blotters after a minute or two, and place them in the dryer, emulsion side up, toward the canvas. If you have no dryer, you can use a blotter roll, available in photo supply stores. Put the prints into the roll with the emulsion toward the fabric, and let them stand until dry.

If you have no established means for drying your prints, or if the *emulsion has been softened by after treatments,* like toning, intensification or reduction, hang them on a string by clothespins, applying one to each corner (the bottom ones serve as weights) and let them dry that way (Fig. 317).

Drying Glossy Prints (Ferrotyping).

Use a ferrotype plate for drying if you made your prints on glossy paper and want them to have a glossy finish. Chromium plated brass ferrotype plates are the most satisfactory. The first step in ferrotyping prints is to wash your hands well with soap and water. Rinse the washed prints in running water, wipe their surfaces *under the water* with your hand, a sponge, or a wad of cotton to remove any dirt or scum that may be on them, then place the prints in a clean tray half filled with water.

Now wash the ferrotype plate. Hold it under running water and wipe it with your open palm. Be careful not to scratch the polished chromium surface of the plate, take your ring off, if you wear one. Place the rinsed ferrotype plate on a table, shiny side up. Do not wipe it. Take the washed prints from the tray of water and place them face down on the ferrotype plate (Fig. 318). Cover the prints with three layers of clean newspaper, and go over this sandwich lightly with a *roller* squeegee (available in photo supply stores). With the other hand hold the end of the newspaper to prevent it

318
Prints are placed on ferrotype plate.

319
Water is squeegeed out from be-tween prints and ferrotype plate, Newspaper on top protects prints and plate, absorbs water.

from slipping (Fig. 319). After you have gone over the whole plate once, go over it again applying *hard* pressure. Be sure that you don't leave out any part. Go over the plate with the roller squeegee twice: lengthwise and cross-wise. Remove the newspapers from the ferrotype plate, the prints are now ready to dry. If you have a dryer, put the plate with the prints into it (the prints are on top), cover it with the canvas and wait until they are completely dry, when the top of the canvas does not feel damp any more to the touch, and, when the canvas is raised, the prints come off the ferrotype plate by themselves, or with gentle helping from you. If the prints are still wet they stick to the plate and will be damaged if you try to force them off.

If you have no dryer just let the ferrotype plate stand undisturbed until the prints peel off by themselves.

Causes of Imperfect Glossy Finish.

Things which can spoil the glossy finish of ferrotyped prints:

Dirty or scratched plates. Never let anything touch the surface of the plate but your bare hand. Don't use a sponge or a cloth to clean it, they may carry hard particles which may scratch the plate. Always keep the plate in its paper bag (in which it came) when not in use. If the bag is torn, make a new one from paper or a soft fabric. Remember that the gloss on your prints cannot be better than that of the plate, and take every precaution to preserve its finish.

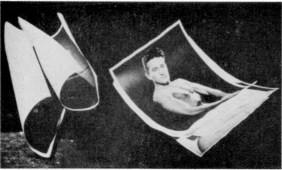

320
Dried prints are usually more or less curled.

321
Curled prints are moistened on the back before they are placed under heavy pressure for 24 hours.

322
Straightened prints lie flat.

Dirty water. In some localities the water supply contains sediment, which harms the plates and prints if it is allowed to accumulate on the prints during washing. Rinse both prints and plate in running water before use.

Insufficient pressure with the squeegee. Apply hard pressure and make sure that you go over the whole plate. If you make a lot of glossy prints it will pay you to get a heavy duty roller squeegee, like the one used by professionals.

Dry prints may stick to the plate if the print or ferrotype plate were not entirely clean, or if the latter is badly scratched. Try soaking them in water, the print may come off that way. Twelve drops of Aerosol or other wetting agent added to every quart of soaking water may help to separate the print from the plate.

Print Straightening.

No matter how you dry your prints, it is likely that they will be more or less curled when dry (Fig. 320). If the prints are to be mounted you don't have to worry about the curling, but if you want to use them without mounting, or in a folder, straightening is necessary.

For straightening you need some device to keep the prints under pressure. This may be a regular print press, sold in photo supply stores, or two wooden boards held together by "C"-clamps, or simply a few large, heavy books.

Take the curled prints and moisten (not wet) their backs with a squeezed out sponge (Fig. 321). Be careful not to moisten the emulsion side. Place the moistened prints face to face and back to back (dry emulsion side toward dry emulsion side and moistened back toward moistened back) and put these prints in the press, between the wooden boards, or under a pile of heavy books. Leave the prints under pressure for 24 hours and they will be flat when you take them out (Fig. 322).

For good results, drying and straightening must be performed with great care.

Mounting Your Pictures

Mounting improves the appearance of any enlargement. Prints are usually mounted on mat boards (sold in photo and art supply stores), but you can also use any other suitable material.

Sometimes the mounting board is completely covered by the print. Usually, however, a margin is left all around. For vertical pictures the margin is made equal on the two sides and on the top, leaving the bottom margin to take care of itself. For a horizontal print on a vertical mount the margins are made equal on the two sides, and the bottom margin is made twice as wide as the top margin.

A somewhat more precise method that makes allowance for the proportions of the print is shown in Fig. 323.

You are under no compulsion to follow either of these methods. They are not laws, they simply explain how prints are usually mounted. If you feel that your picture sits more comfortably on the mount with somewhat different spacing, be guided by your own good judgment.

We would suggest, however, that you avoid extreme departures from common practice, such as placing the print in one corner of the mount. The purpose of the mount is to give the picture space in which to be seen. Radical mountings call attention to the mount instead of the picture.

Mounting with Rubber Cement.

You can mount your prints rather easily with *rubber cement*. Its advantage is easy handling, its disadvantage is that it is not permanent. In time the enlargement will peel off the mount. If it does, however, it can be remounted with another application of the rubber cement.

Rubber cement can be bought in photo or art supply stores. If fresh, use it as it comes, if it gets too thick on standing, use rubber cement thinner to dilute it. Be careful, both rubber cement and thinner are inflammable.

Apply rubber cement with a good quality varnish brush, which is kept in the rubber cement all the time to prevent it from drying out. The container for the rubber cement must be kept closed when not in use.

If the print is to be trimmed, do it first, then place it on the mount and measure out the margins. When the print is in its proper position on the

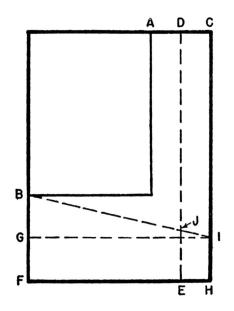
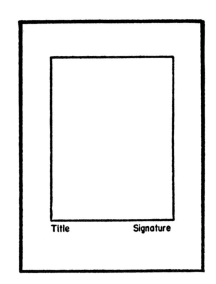

323 The preferred placement of prints on their mounts is usually in a position somewhat above center with equal side margins. This position is usually found by trial and error, which frequently leads to poor placement of prints upon their mounts, especially where prints vary in size.

A geometric method which places the print very nearly upon "optical center" regardless of its size and shape is shown in the diagram.

Step 1: Trim the print to size and place it in the upper lefthand corner of the mount, its top right and lower left corners falling at A and B respectively.

Step 2: Divide the remaining space A to C in half to locate point D, then draw the line D to E parallel to the edge of the mount.

Step 3: Divide the remaining space B to F between the bottom of the print and mount in half, locating point G, then draw the line G to I parallel to the bottom of the mount.

Step 4: Connect points B and I. The intersection of this line with the line DE gives the point J.

Step 5: Mount print, with its right edge on line DE, and the lower right corner on point J.

   Title and signature are usually placed as shown in the righthand figure.

From PHOTO-LAB-INDEX, Copyright 1951, Morgan & Lester, by permission of copyright owners.

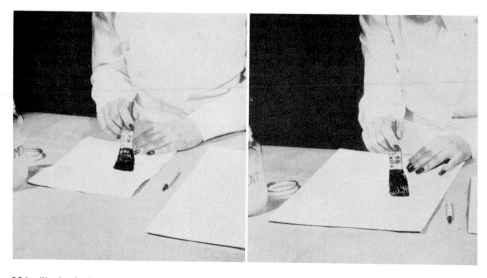

324 The back of the print is covered with rubber **325** Rubber cement is spread on the mount.
cement.

mount, take a pencil and draw a line on the mount all around the print. This line will show you how far to spread the rubber cement on the mount and will also help you to place the print for the actual mounting.

Take the print and cover the back with the rubber cement thinly, but completely (Fig. 324). Put the print aside and cover the mount with the rubber cement (Fig. 325) according to the markings previously made, spreading the rubber cement about ½ inch beyond the markings. This will insure good adhesion at the edges of the print and the excess can be easily removed afterwards. Simply rub it off with your fingers after it is dry. You have to let the rubber cement dry completely on both print and mount, which takes about 10 minutes. When they are dry you can do the mounting.

Place the mount in front of you, pick up the print and hold it above the mount. Lower the *top edge* of the print and carefully place it on the mount, matching the edge of the print with the pencil line previously made. During this operation the other hand holds the rest of the print in the air (Fig. 326). This is necessary because if you lay the whole print on the mount it will stick and you could not move the print to its proper position according to the markings. When the top edge is in place lay the rest of the print on the mount. If the top edge was placed properly, the markings should correspond to the edges of the print all around.

Take a piece of clean wrapping paper, place it on the print and apply hard ressure with the roller squeegee on top of this paper (Fig. 327) both

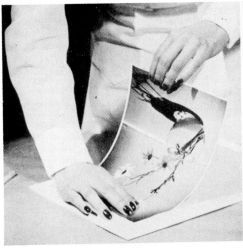

326 The top of the print is lined up with the markings on the mount.

327 The mounted print is squeegeed through a piece of wrapping paper.

lengthwise and crosswise. Then rub the mount with your dry (and clean) finger where there is excess rubber cement (Fig. 328). The dry rubber cement rubs off easily. The mounting is now complete.

Mounting With Dry Mounting Tissue.

A more permanent method for mounting photographs is with dry mounting tissue. For dry mounting you need a supply of dry mounting tissue, a tacking iron (sold in photo supply stores) and a household electric iron with automatic heat control or a dry mounting press.

Plug in the tacking iron and let it heat for about 10 minutes, then take one sheet of mounting tissue, place it on the back of the untrimmed print, and gently rub it with the hot tacking iron in the center (Fig. 329). The tissue will stick to the print where you touched it with the hot iron. If the tissue sticks to the iron rather than to the print, it means that the iron is not hot enough. After the mounting tissue is tacked to the middle of the print, trim around the print and the tissue together, then lay the print on the mount and measure the margins. When the print is positioned on the mount properly, place one hand on the center of the print to prevent it from slipping, then turn up one corner of the *print only* (not the tissue), and tack the corner of the tissue to the mount (Fig. 330). Repeat this on each corner.

Now the print is ready for mounting. Put it into the mounting press, if you have one, and follow the instructions supplied with it. If you have no mounting press, a household electric iron with automatic heat control will

328
Excess rubber cement is rubbed off.

serve just as well. Put a sheet of clean, heavy wrapping paper on the print, and place the heated iron on the wrapping paper (Fig. 331). The automatic heat control of the iron is to be set to "rayon" or "low." *Keep the iron in motion all the time* and go over the print several times, then put aside the iron and the wrapping paper, take a clean handkerchief or similar soft material and go over the print with that, applying pressure until the print has cooled off somewhat.

To test the mounting, bend the mount slightly in each direction. If bending loosens the print, mount it again, giving the tissue enough time to heat and stick.

On humid days iron the wrapping paper for a few seconds before you put it on top of the print, otherwise they may stick together.

Mount your prints to make them more presentable and more permanent.

329 Dry mounting tissue is tacked to the center of the print.　　**330** Corner of tissue is tacked to the mount.　　**331** Mounting is done with household iron.

Print Finishing

On close examination of your print you will probably notice several small light or dark spots which do not belong there. The light spots are usually caused by dust on the negative or on the enlarging paper during exposure, the dark ones by pinholes or deep scratches in the negative.

The picture itself may contain small areas which are too dark or too light, like a portrait printed from an unretouched negative, for example, with blemishes, freckles, wrinkles, etc. spoiling the appearance of the picture.

Retouching will help you to remove the undesired light or dark spots from your prints. There are only two basic steps in print retouching: some parts are to be darkened, others are to be lightened. Figs. 332 to 335 show the basic defects that you will encounter on a print: sharply defined lighter areas (Fig. 332), gradually fading lighter areas (Fig. 333), sharply defined darker areas (Fig. 334), and gradually fading darker areas (Fig. 335). These examples are exaggerated and simplified for the sake of illustration.

Materials Needed.

You need the following materials for retouching:

Kodak Spotting Colors. This includes three small white plastic sheets covered with colors: black, sepia (brown), and white.

Two bottles of "Spotone," one #1, blue, and one #2, reddish brown. These are to be mixed with the spotting colors, when needed, for work on

332, 333, 334, 335 Simplified examples of print defects.

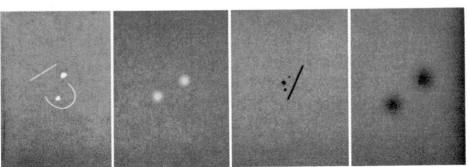

blue and selenium toned prints.

Some sort of small glass water container (whiskey glass, ashtray, etc.).

Pencils: 4H and H lead pencils. Additional hardness grades (7H, HB) are useful. Lead pencils leave a shiny mark on the print, buy carbon pencils for use on matte prints. Carbon pencils are sold in art supply stores. Get a B, an H and an HH. Instead of regular pencils you may buy a lead holder and separate leads, available in art stores.

One #4 and one #3 good quality round *sable* brushes (Winsor & Newton or other good make).

One DiCarlo Crystal Etcher (available through your photo dealer or directly from George Murphy, Inc.) This knife is the easiest to maintain, it needs no sharpening. When it gets dull the point can be replaced. Other etching knives can be used if you know how to keep them very sharp.

A jar of Kodak Black Opaque.

Small sheets of lintless photographic blotters.

Small sheets of white writing paper.

Small sheets of fine sandpaper.

Setting Up for Work.

We describe a simplified method of print retouching. It works well and it is easy to learn. Three basic methods of correction are used: 1. Spotting colors applied with brush. Can be used on prints made on any photographic paper. 2. Spotting with pencil. Can be used on matte or semi-matte papers only. Glossy or other shiny surfaces do not "take" the pencil. 3. Lightening areas with an etching knife. Will work with all but the rough surface papers.

Fig. 336 shows the basic working setup on a table: The small water container, spotting colors, a piece of lintless blotter, a white paper, and the print to be spotted. You need good illumination coming from the left (from the

337 Brush is dipped into water.   **338** Excess water is removed on blotter.

right if you are left handed) or from behind you. Light coming from above or from in front of you will cause disturbing reflections on the print.

Loading the Brush with Spotting Color.

The most common faults you will have to correct on the prints are small light spots, usually caused by dust on the negative and/or on the enlarging paper during exposure under the enlarger. To remove them follow these steps: dip the larger brush in the water (Fig. 337). Remove excess water from the brush on the blotter (Fig. 338). Load the brush with the spotting color (Fig. 339). Twist the brush during loading to get the color evenly distributed all around.

Work the color evenly into the brush by moving it over the white paper with a *continuous twisting-pulling* motion (Fig. 340.) This step is important, it serves a triple purpose: first, it distributes the color in the brush evenly, second, it shapes the brush into a fine point, and third, it gives you a chance to check the tone of the color in the brush, which should be the same as the tone of the print area surrounding the to be removed light spot. If the color in the brush is too light, pick up more color from the disk, if it is too dark, dip the point of the brush in the water and try it again on the white paper.

If the spotting color does not match the color of the print, as it may not when you retouch a toned print, for example, you can make it match by mixing the spotting color with that from the brown disk, or with one of the Spotone dyes.

Spotting with the Brush.

To do the actual spotting carry the properly loaded brush over the area to be spotted, hold it about one inch above the paper, then *lightly touch the*

179

339 Brush is loaded with spotting color.　　**340** Color in brush is checked on white paper.

spot with the POINT of the brush. If properly done the point of the brush will not bend, it will just leave a tiny spot of color on the print. *The purpose of spotting is to cover the to be darkened area with adjacent tiny dots, not* to "paint" the area with the brush.

Using Fig. 332 as an example, Fig. 341 shows the proper way of touching the to be spotted area with the point of the brush. Fig. 342 shows the brush in the raised position, ready to be lowered again to make the next dot.

341-342　Motion to be performed with brush during spotting.

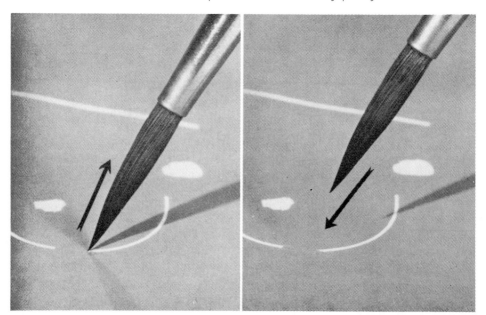

343
Close up of spot which has been touched out. To identify notice spot in Fig. 342 which is missing here.

Fig. 343 is a greatly enlarged picture of a retouched spot. This enlarged view clearly shows that the retouched area is made up of dots. The magnified image looks rather uneven, but in natural size the retouching cannot be detected by a casual viewer.

Don't look too closely at a spot during retouching, definitely not through a magnifying glass. Look at the print from natural viewing distance during work.

If the spotted area appears to be too dark you can do one of two things: First, you can "tickle" the dark spot with the point of the etching knife. Just tickle, don't scrape. This will remove the excess spotting color and the spotted area will match the surrounding. Second, you can remove the color completely and start anew. To remove the color wrap a clean white handkerchief around your finger and dip it in the water (Fig. 344). Remove excess water by a touch on the blotter (Fig. 345), then wipe the spot off the print with a short

344 Clean cloth is dipped into water.

345 Excess water is removed on blotter.

346 Spoiled spotting is wiped off.

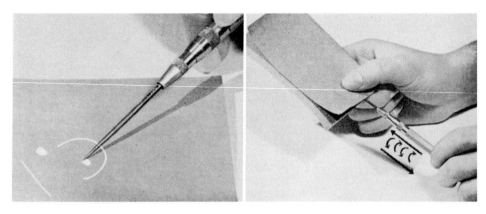

347 Spotting with pencil.   **348** Pencil is sharpened for spotting.

sweep of the wet cloth (Fig. 346). Do not press hard and do not go over the spot twice. If all color is not removed with one sweep, start again, using a clean part of the handkerchief.

Spotting with the Pencil.

Spotting can also be done with a pencil if the area on which the spot is located is not too dark (Fig. 347). The to be darkened area is covered with fine pencil lines until it disappears. Use a hard pencil (7H, 4H) on light areas, softer ones (H, HB) on darker areas. Both lead and carbon pencils are used the same way. Don't press the pencil hard. If it does not take, use brush and spotting colors. Keep twisting the pencil during work. The point wears smooth fast and it will slip. Twisting changes the position of the point, keeps it "toothed."

To get a fine point on your pencil: strip the wood off 3 inches of lead (or pull out about 3 inches of lead from your lead holder). Insert the lead in a folded sheet of sand paper and with one hand hold the point of the lead between your fingers *through* the sand paper, while the other hand moves the pencil with a simultaneous twisting and pushing-pulling motion (Fig. 348).

Etching Out Dark Spots.

Dark spots are to be removed by etching. Take the DiCarlo Crystal Etcher and *gently shave off* the top of the emulsion until the tone is sufficiently lightened. The etcher is to be held over the spot at an angle, the curved edge just touching the paper. To etch you simply move the knife in one direction, from right to left over the paper (Fig. 349), slightly lifting it for the backward stroke. Do not press the knife down, don't "dig in." The properly handled knife shaves off the top of the emulsion evenly and a small group of shavings

349 Position of etching knife for removing dark spot.

350 Properly used etching knife gradually shaves off dark spot, shavings collect in front of knife.

will collect in front of it (Fig. 350). Blow away the shavings when they start to obscure the spot you are working on. Other etching knives work the same way, but they must be very sharp, otherwise they scratch the emulsion, instead of shaving it.

You can correct an over etched or unevenly etched area with the pencil. The etched part of the print has a "tooth," it takes pencil retouching very well on any paper. Brush and spotting color can also be used.

Removing Pinholes.

Very dark spots on the print, caused by so-called pinholes in the negative, cannot be etched out as described. These spots go too deep, they must be "dug out" with the point of the knife. Dig out the black spot, then fill in the remaining white spot with pencil or brush.

Another way to remove dark spots is with light spotting color. Kodak Spotting Colors contain a white disk, which can be mixed with other colors to match the surrounding area of the dark spot. This mixture is then used to lighten the too dark area.

You can prevent black spots on the print by removing pinholes from the negative before enlarging. It is easy to do. Fig. 351 shows a pinhole in a negative, probably caused by dust on the film when the picture was taken. On the print this would cause a black spot. To remove the pinhole the negative is placed so that it can be viewed by transmitted light, then Kodak Black Opaque is applied over the pinhole with a finely pointed brush (Fig. 352). The resulting black spot on the negative (Fig. 353) will become a white spot on the print, which can be spotted out easily.

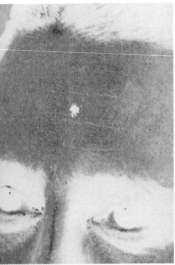 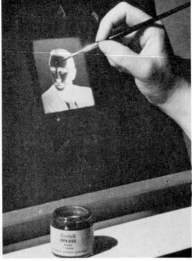 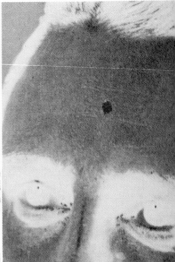

351 Pinhole in negative.

352 Pinhole is covered with opaque.

353 Opaqued pinhole will make white spot on print which can be spotted out with pencil or brush.

Varnishing.

Sometimes your finished prints appear to be rather dull, you would like them to have more brilliance. Varnishing dull prints with Kodak Print Lustre will give them more sparkle.

Apply the varnish according to instructions on the bottle. Do not use Kodak Print Lustre on prints which have been spotted with a pencil, because it will take off the pencil work.

184

Cash For Your Prints

You can use your newly acquired knowledge of enlarging as a source of income.

If you are a professional photographer, the better prints you make, the more you can charge for them.

Making quality enlargements will not only help you to advance as a photographer, you can also cash in on it directly. You can make money with enlarging either by taking a job as a printer, or you can make enlargements for others on your own. The latter is especially adaptable for part time work.

There is a great potential market for quality enlargements. Amateur photographers, who for some reason cannot or will not do their own darkroom work, are always eager to have custom made enlargements. They are willing to pay well, as long as they get what they want. There are very few places in the entire country where such work is done, all you have to do is to spread around the word that you do quality enlarging and the work will come in, probably more than you can handle. Local photo supply stores, camera clubs and other organizations are good places to look for work.

Professional photographers are also potential customers. Turning out enlargements fast enough is a constant headache for most photo studios, small or large. When work is held up, especially during rush periods, you usually find the bottleneck in the printing room. If you offer them your services for making quality enlargements, you will be surprised how eagerly most of them will accept. Of course, you cannot get work from professionals if you do photographic work yourself and they can expect to lose customers to you. You have to specialize in enlarging to be patronized by photographers.

Your prices for enlargements depend on the quality of the work you do. You don't have to compete with the prices of "drug store" enlargements if you do better work. The best way to figure out how much you can charge is on an hourly basis: figure out how long it takes for you to make an enlargement, charge a good hourly wage plus the cost of materials. This means that your prices should vary accordingly to the work necessary to make each enlargement.

Professionals will pay less than amateurs, because of the larger quantity of work they give you, but don't let them cut your prices too low, as they are likely to do if you give them the chance.

If you want to cash in on your knowledge of quality enlarging, keep these points in mind: Get organized so that you can turn out the work without wasted time and effort. Always do your best, don't compromise on quality. Don't be afraid to charge a fair price, based on the time spent in making the enlargement.

High quality work turned out in satisfactory quantities at fair prices will mean a steady and sizeable income to you, making photographic enlarging a lucrative business or a profitable sideline.

CHAPTER TWENTY-FOUR

Summary

Books on enlarging usually end with a collection of pictures which are supposed to show how the techniques described in the book can be put to use. We were seriously tempted to include such a collection, but after considering the possible effects, we didn't do it.

This is a book on enlarging techniques, with the emphasis on craftsmanship. Regardless of what kind of work you prefer to do, you can utilize the enlarging procedures described. No matter what examples we might have shown to demonstrate the usefulness of those procedures, many of you would have said: "Why should I learn *that* technique? I don't want to make *that* kind of picture."

To prevent such reactions, to avoid the chance of limiting the usefulness of the techniques described, we decided not to include examples in the summary.

However, in the course of explaining the enlarging procedures, we had to include examples all along. Don't take these as typical examples of the results that can be accomplished by the techniques with which they are used. Any one of the methods described is suitable for use in any kind of print making, regardless of the type of work you do. This is very important. You must consider each technique in the light of your own work, your own requirements, regardless of the type of picture we happened to use as an example to demonstrate the technique. At times you will have to do considerable thinking in order to figure out how to print a negative exactly the way you want to print it, but you will find that regardless of the problems involved, one or more of the described techniques will enable you to get the result you want.

The emphasis is on "you will have to do considerable thinking." You can get top notch results only if you give serious thought to what you have to do. Each and every print you make is a challenge, calling for all you have in the way of imagination, creative ability and craftsmanship.

You have to draw on your own resources for imagination and creative ability, for craftsmanship you have to study this book. We repeat, you have to *study* it. Don't just read it as if it were a novel, it makes rather poor reading that way. Instead, take it into your darkroom and *do* each technique as described. The results you get will make the book exciting reading, you will be anxious to go on and learn more. You may, and probably will have difficulties, their seriousness depending on your previous experience in enlarging. Don't let these difficulties make you disappointed or disgusted. Remember, that at one time or another, you have learned everything that you now know. Much of it is surely more difficult to master than enlarging. If you proceed with diligence you will be producing fine prints within a short time.

Index